FASHION
SOURCE
BOOK

FASHION SOURCE BOOK

AMY DE LA HAYE

THE WELLFLEET PRESS
WELLFLEET

A QUARTO BOOK

Copyright © 1988 Quarto Publishing plc

Published by Wellfleet Press,
110, Enterprise Avenue,
Secaucus, New Jersey 07094

ISBN 1-55521-339-1

This book was designed and produced by
Quarto Publishing plc
The Old Brewery, 6 Blundell Street
London N7 9BH

Senior editor   Henrietta Wilkinson
Designer   John Grain
Picture researchers   Jan Croot, Cindy Greenslade, Joanna Wiese

Art director   Moira Clinch
Editorial director   Carolyn King

Typeset by Burbeck Associates Ltd
Manufactured in Hong Kong by Regent Publishing Services Ltd
Printed by Leefung-Asco Printers Ltd, Hong Kong

FOREWORD

*"The glass of fashion and the
mould of form,
The observ'd of all the
observers."*

HAMLET, ACT III, SCENE 1, LINE 161

This book has aimed, within the brevity of its text, to discuss the consumption, production and retailing of fashion, and ultimately to consider garment design itself. Although the century's leading couturiers do appear, a broader analysis has also been made of the dress available to all social classes. This is in stark contrast to the majority of dress histories, which almost exclusively focus upon haute couture, and the collection policy of most museums with their emphasis on the rare and precious. This selection of the superlative too often distorts our view of history, so that we inevitably accept the images of Schiaparelli and Dior as representative of their time. In reality, couture is available to a minority only, and thus to gain a truer perspective we should also look at everyday clothing. The methods of design dissemination, from the most luxurious couture dress to the cheapest rayon one, have been discussed in the main introduction.

The bulk of this book is pictorial. While the glossy photographs of couture garments on mannequins epitomize an ideal, everyday photographs have also been used extensively to provide a balanced view. Few, if any, of these have appeared in other books. Thus they provide vital source material for the dress historian or designer and are a delight to the interested fashion consumer.

Amy de la Haye.

MA (RCA)

CONTENTS

8

INTRODUCTION

16

CHAPTER ONE

1900
TO
1908

46

CHAPTER·THREE

1920
TO
1929

32

CHAPTER·TWO

1909
TO
1919

64

CHAPTER·FOUR

1930
TO
1939

80
CHAPTER·FIVE
1940
TO
1949

120
CHAPTER·SEVEN
1960
TO
1969

166
CHAPTER·NINE
1980s

98
CHAPTER·SIX
1950
TO
1959

144
CHAPTER·EIGHT
1970
TO
1979

188
INDEX

192
BIBLIOGRAPHY AND CREDITS

INTRODUCTION

The Paris couture industry was founded by Charles Frederick Worth, who opened his premises at 7, rue de la Paix, Paris, in 1858. In succeeding from the generally anonymous dressmaker and tailor of the time, he was to become the first highly acclaimed designer, who dictated what his customers wore. He started his career as an apprentice to the drapery trade in London, moving to Paris at the age of 22, where he dressed his wife in clothes that he designed and made himself. His opening came when he persuaded the rich and influential Princess Pauline de Metternich, wife of the Austrian ambassador, to wear one of his garments to a ball at the Court of Napoleon III. It was much admired, and Worth was soon dressing the Empress Eugénie, Napoleon III's wife, her ladies-in-waiting and visiting members of the foreign aristocracy. He was also patronized by women of the demi-monde and the new industrial millionaires' wives, who clamored to live and dress in the same style as those with landed wealth; the elaborate crinolines that Worth designed for these women are inseparable from the luxury and extravagance associated with the Second Empire. It is interesting, however, that although Worth became the great arbiter of

Punch cartoon, July 4, 1863, The Haunted Lady, or The Ghost in the Looking Glass. Madame La Modiste: "We would not have disappointed your ladyship, at any sacrifice, and the robe is finished." The woman in the mirror is the exhausted dressmaker. Punch regularly highlighted the plight of clothing workers during these years.

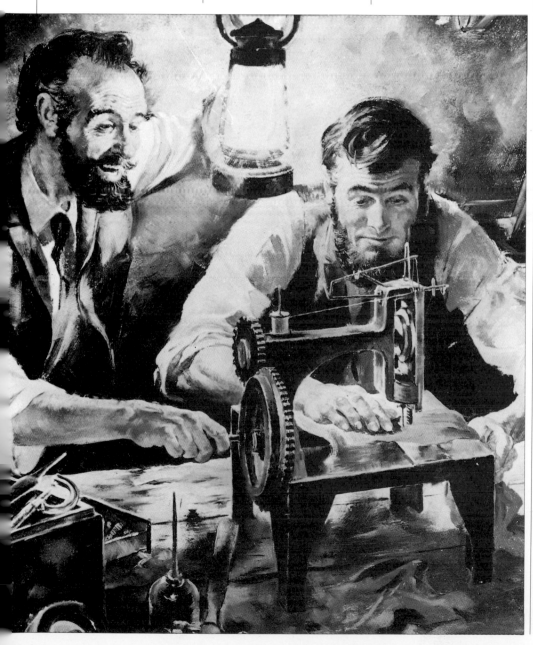

Romanticized painting of two tailors working with a Singer sewing machine. Singer became the major manufacturer of sewing machines from the mid nineteenth century onward. The reality was appalling working conditions, long hours and pathetically low wages.

taste in dress, he did not enjoy the high social status which leading designers enjoy today. Despite the fact that fashion was widely accepted to be an art, its makers were regarded as tradespeople and did not mix socially with their customers.

Couture for the rich

The Parisian couture industry became established around Worth's premises and the neighboring Place Vendôme (where it is located to this day), and many subsidiary but vitally important trades — such as specialist beading and embroidery workshops, and luxury ribbon and button makers — also surfaced to feed the burgeoning couture houses. By 1900, the most successful of these were employing up to 1,000 workers and exporting nearly two-thirds of all their model gowns. Creative talent in the form of fine artists, writers and designers had always flocked to Paris, and throughout the nineteenth and twentieth-centuries, artists and fashion designers often combined forces to achieve the most spectacular results. Among the many twentieth-century examples are the heads with long wispy hair drawn by Jean Cocteau for Schiaparelli to have embroidered onto her garments, and the magnificent costumes which Chanel designed for the Ballets Russes' performance of *Le Train Bleu* in 1924.

From the days of Worth until the 1930s, Paris and fashion became synonymous, its supremacy virtually unchallenged. In part, this was due to the French government, who always encouraged the arts (including fashion) which contributed considerably to their economy: in Britain and the United States, on the other hand, this support system never existed to the same extent. American haute couture was essentially a wholesale enterprise (while French and British couture houses were retail concerns) with many of their couturiers — including Hattie Carnegie and Nettie Rosenstein — selling their fashions through department stores, such as Lord and Taylor and Bergdorf Goodman, during the 1930s. The former of these stores was particularly progressive in 1932 when it advertised dresses that were designed and made in the United States. Although many American couturiers were immensely successful, their clothes often bore the name of the store through which they were sold and the designers themselves remained anonymous. As the department stores had always promoted their allegiance with Paris, it was often implied that the designers of their clothes were all of French origin, thus reinforcing Paris's grip on fashion.

During the 1930s, Hollywood did exert some influence upon popular fashion and British couturier Norman Hartnell's clothing for royalty was widely admired. Generally, however, what was created in Paris remained the last word in fashion. Wealthy women from all over the world bought their garments from Paris, and the middle

Left
Luxurious ballgown by the House of Worth, c. 1900.

Right
Fashion plate from the American magazine Godey's, c. 1870. Bustles were very fashionable during the 1870s and 80s – although Flora Thompson's poor community did not adopt them until the 1880s, when they were considered the very latest in style.

Far right
Expensive visiting costume, 1902. At this date fashion revelled in luxury.

GODEY'S FASHIONS.
FOR DESCRIPTION SEE FASHION DEPARTMENT.

classes, unable to afford couture clothes, patronized dressmakers and department stores where they could obtain cheaper versions. Couture garments were — and indeed are today — available to only a tiny fraction of the population, perhaps less than one percent, but while the number of these fashions was not significant, they were most important stylistically. From the 1920s onwards, their designs disseminated down to the cheapest levels of clothing.

Dress for the poor

Up until that time, fashion had been the prerogative of the rich and leisured. The limited income of, and hard daily work undertaken by, working class women meant that their clothing had to be comfortable and durable. High fashion fulfilled neither of these requirements. Apart from the financial restrictions, a crinoline or hobble skirt would have been utterly impractical. Thus, the rather shapeless garments made from humble fabrics which these women wore clearly reflected their financial constraints. A

fashionable appearance could sometimes be achieved within communities, but these were markedly behind the styles displayed by high society. In her memoirs, Flora Thompson[1] describes how the agricultural women in the isolated hamlet in Oxfordshire, where she was brought up during the 1880s, used to roll up pieces of fabric like cushions and wear them under their frocks to give the impression of bustles — which were high fashion during the 1870s. These women were aware of fashion — albeit slightly out of date — and made what concessions they could to achieve it.

Working-class men's and children's clothing could be bought ready made from the mid-nineteenth century, following the advent of the sewing machine, invented in the United States by Elias Howe in 1846. There had been many attempts to design a sewing machine since the middle of the eighteenth century, but Howe was the first to produce a working model. Due to the standardized nature of men's and children's clothes, manufacturers could produce them in bulk without worrying about fashion changes.

1880   1890   1895   1900   1910

Furthermore, they had a large and assured market as few women could tailor a man's suit, although they could often make many of their children's clothes. In general, from 1900 onwards, men had just one suit which was worn for "best" and at weekends, the design of which was fairly static until after World War II. Indeed, it was not until the 1950s that the majority of men's clothing was truly influenced by fashion.

Ready-made fashion for all

The single most important development in twentieth-century dress was that fashion became widely available in the form of ready-made clothes. From the 1920s onwards many couturiers designed styles which could be worn by active, hard-working women as well as by a rich elite. In contrast to the production of men's and children's clothing, however, women's off-the-peg wear was produced on a small scale, providing both individuality of design and insurance against fashion misjudgments.

Then, as now, manufacturers of women's fashion clothing obtained their designs from two sources. The first was the purchase of fashion forecasts, which illustrated the forthcoming season's designs, textiles and colors; and the second and most widely used method was the direct copying of couture or *prêt-à-porter* garments, which were then adapted for the mass market. This practice reached its peak during the interwar years, when fashion was more rigid than it is today and designs came almost exclusively from Paris.

The direct copying of couture models was undertaken by the top end of the clothing trade — that is, at department store level. Although store representatives did visit Paris with the express intention of purchasing prototypes and buying models or toiles for this purpose, most copying was unofficial. Lillian Farley, a mannequin for the couturier Patou during the 1920s, describes how his models were copied: "They bought little and would ask to see a model over and over again: always in a group of four or five. It was well known that each one would memorize a certain part of the dress, one studying the sleeve details, another the skirt and still another the trimmings. Back at the hotel they would make an accurate sketch of the model to be copied at home."[2] These were then sent by ship or plane to the East End of London or to Seventh Avenue in New York and within days replica dresses would appear in all the shops. The cheaper end of the trade, unable to visit Paris themselves, would in turn copy the top end's version. By these means, the design of the most luxurious couture model eventually filtered down to the cheapest rayon dress.

Edna Woolman Chase, a leading American couturier and editor of American *Vogue* from 1914-1952, went so far as to state that this was "... an international spy system to turn the military green with envy." Some manufacturers even sewed facsimile labels of leading Paris houses into their garments

to give the impression that they were originals. This association with Paris imbued a garment with added desirability and could often command a higher price than the same garment without one. The copying and diluting of couture garments for the mass market has continued to this day, only now New York, London and Milan are also recognized capitals of fashion.

Retail outlets

An inevitable consequence of the off-the-peg mass market was the development of the retail clothing outlet. Ready-made clothing for men, women and children is available from three types of outlet: the department store, the small-scale unit retailer and chain stores. Department stores have always stocked top-quality items, and during the nineteenth century were exclusively patronized by the middle and upper classes. As the twentieth century progressed, they recognized and responded to the changing and broadening nature of the market. In the 1920s, for example, Selfridges opened an immensely successful bargain basement, and during the 1960s introduced Miss Selfridge to entice the fashion conscious teenager to spend her earnings.

Top Left Marks & Spencer garberdine suit, Summer 1988.

Above
Mary Quant has generally been credited for opening the first "boutique," Bazaar, in Great Britain in 1955. Here, is the footwear she launched.

Above

Marks & Spencer's "inexpensive frocks", c. 1933. This shows a trial window display, copies of which were sent to all branches of the store to ensure identical displays. Priced at 2s/11d, these were among the cheapest ready made dresses available. The basic design is the same, but they are differentiated by the use of different fabrics, collar shapes, belts and buttons.

But it has been the small-scale unit retailer that has dominated the fashion market throughout most of this century. Their strength lies in the personal contact between the customer and the owner, and in the limited quantity of merchandise on display, which implies an exclusive design. The small retailer flourished during the interwar years, providing an outlet for the flood of fashion clothing which swamped the market, and reached its peak again during the 1960s with the "boutique revolution."

The late 1920s and early 1930s saw chain stores, such as Marks & Spencer in Great Britain, introduce ready-made clothing to their stocks of household goods. The design of their garments was "safe," neither in the forefront nor lagging behind contemporary fashion. Marks & Spencer achieved commercial success by defining an area of the market which did not seek high fashion, but preferred to benefit instead from good value, quality garments which their large scale production made possible. The 1980s are witnessing the rise of a new type of chain, such as the Next stores, which sell limited quantities of fashionable, quality garments. They have also revitalized and upgraded the mail order business.

[1] (*Lark Rise to Candleford,* London, Oxford University Press, 1945, p94.)
[2] (Chase, Edna Woolman and Chase, Ilka, *Always in Vogue,* Victor Gollancz Ltd, London, 1954, pp166-7.)

Camille Clifford, 1906. Her hour-glass curves epitomized the fashionable ideal.

CHAPTER·ONE
1900
TO
1908

"The Edwardian age was a period of gaiety, when life was so inexpensive that a dandy with four hundred pounds a year could go out dancing most nights of the week, wearing lavender gloves and a wired button-hole in the lapel of his tail-coat."[1]

From 1900-1907 rich men and women dressed in a tremendous variety of clothing for different occasions —at great expense. For example, a weekend away involved as many as 16 complete changes of outfit, including hats, gloves, shoes and jewelry. Separate ensembles were worn during the morning, afternoon and evening, and likewise for specific occasions and activities, such as garden parties and balls, walking, riding, golf and motoring. Completely different sets were also required for town and country wear. Numerous books on etiquette appeared on the market to guide the uncertain on the correct modes of behavior and dress for these myriad social events. The author of *Etiquette for Men* advised those who were in the city out of season that, "In August and September society people are not supposed to be in town, you can wear country clothes — a light thin lounge suit and a straw hat. If you are in town in August and September, you are supposed to be there only because you are passing through on your way to the country."[2]

Throughout this period the restrictive and elaborate clothing that rich women wore signified their wealth and leisure. In his famous sociological survey *The Theory of the Leisure Class* (1899), Thorstein Veblen stressed that couture clothing was the most blatant form of conspicuous consumption, and that body-compressing corsets were worn for the purpose of lowering the subject's vitality and rendering her completely unfit for any strenuous activity: "It is true, the corset impairs the personal attraction of the wearer, but the loss suffered on that score is offset by the gain in reputability which comes from her visibly increased expensiveness and infirmity."[3]

At the other end of society, Robert Roberts describes his memories of growing up amidst a poor background at the

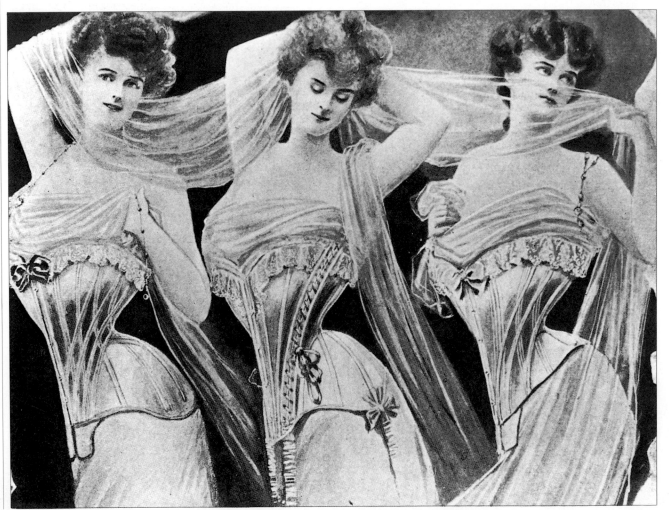

Left
The Edwardian S-bend corset achieved the desirable shape shown here by distorting the spine and compressing the waist and abdomen. Padding often assisted the fashionably top-heavy silhouette.

Right
Queen Alexandra was noted for the promotion of pearl chokers; they emphasized her elegant long neck, and also disguised a birthmark that was said to embarrass her.

beginning of the century, shrewdly observing that prestige was not automatically inflated by proofs of affluence. "Nelly," he writes, "for all her fancy boa, frocks and jewellery, stayed 'ruined' while the temporary flushes of thieves served only to lower their status further."[4]

The back room of Roberts' family shop was used as a depot for goods under the custody of the pawnbroker. In poor Edwardian society, position was not judged solely by what one possessed, but also by what one pawned. Roberts describes how people were thankful to have spare clothing to pledge in return for cash for food so that they could avoid pawning goods from the home, such as bed linen and kitchen utensils.

During the early years of the twentieth century the Parisian couture houses of Paquin, Callot Soeurs, Drecoll, Doucet and Worth led international fashion. The prestigious house of Worth was run by Jean Philippe and Gaston, the two sons of the founder, who had died in 1895. the daughters and wives of wealthy American plutocrats were great customers of the Paris couture trade and between 1879 and 1914 American society, which worshipped European culture, increasingly married into the British aristocracy. In 1907, *The Gentlewoman* magazine announced the marriage of Miss Padelford and the Hon Bertie Grosvenor, stating that this added "...yet another American-born lady to the ranks of future English peeresses." These women, who became known as the Dollar Princesses, gained a highly sought after title and the families received a fortune in the form of a dowry.

The fashions designed by Lady Duff-Gordon, under the trade-name of Lucille, were immensely popular in Great Britain. In the mid 1890s she was the first couturier to hold an entertaining fashion parade in the vein that we are accustomed to today. Live models had only just been introduced at this date, replacing sawdust and wax dummies.

As no society women would consider modeling gowns, Lucille sought six young girls from the middle and lower-middle classes of South London to perform this role. Lucille is an isolated example of a British dressmaker who created individual styles, whereas most, such as Jays and Redfern, adhered strictly to Paris dictates. Rumor had it that the 17-year-old Lady Clarendon had secured her marriage to a very eligible husband by wearing a gray satin Lucille dress. As a result, Lucille, who was already highly successful, became considered lucky and was widely patronized by debutantes. She was also the pioneer of glamorous underwear.

For those who could not afford, but had aspirations to possess, Paris couture, Kate Newton of Great Portland Street, London, advertised that her establishment regularly received consignments of "exhibited" gowns from the leading aforementioned houses at just one-fifth of the original price. The cost of a couture garment is the private

Above
It became the vogue in the 1900s for women to take up sports with a vengeance. They still had to contend with long and heavy skirts and restrictive corseting, however.

Left
An extravagant design of 1902, trimmed with chinchilla fur and lace.

agreement between the maker and customer, and is rarely divulged. Women's magazines often included a "Private Exchange" section, through which women could sell and buy slightly worn garments. This was particularly useful for mourning dress, generally worn for a brief period only.

Vogue has become the dominant fashion magazine of the twentieth century. This was founded in 1892 and bought by the publisher Condé Nast in 1909. During the 1900s, 10s and 20s fashion was photographed, but this was considered to be an inferior medium to drawing: *Vogue* did not use a photograph on its cover until 1932. Actors, actresses, dancers and society women frequently modeled clothing, whereas since World War II *Vogue* has almost exclusively used professional models.

From the 1890s to 1914 the American illustrator Charles Dana Gibson exerted a tremendous influence upon women's dress. His "Gibson Girl" character first appeared on the pages of *Life* and *Colliers,* and did much to aid women's emancipation during the period. The Gibson Girl was illustrated playing golf, swimming, riding and bicycling, she was independent and stood tall and proud, often overwhelming the presence of any men she was drawn with; she wore long, tailored skirts and blouses with an S-bend corset, which thrust the top half of her body forward (giving women the tightly upholstered looking mono bosom which characterized these years); and so popular was she, that by the turn of the century, wallpaper covered with Gibson Girl heads was marketed for bachelors. Because she was always illustrated with clean shaven men mustaches went out of fashion. Whereas maturity was the keynote of most Edwardian fashion, the Gibson Girl was youthful, and the blouses which she popularized (intricately embroidered, faggoted, pintucked and often with a lace insert,) introduced separates into women's wardrobes.

However, these items were frequently made by sweated labor in Europe and America, and factory conditions were often appalling, as were those of home- and outwork. In Great Britain the *Daily News* Sweated Trades Exhibition of 1906 highlighted the plight of many of the trade's home workers, among the lowest paid of whom were the shirt and blouse makers. White flannel shirts were made for a penny each, and a dozen of these took 14-15 hours to make. Throughout the twentieth century, out and home workers have coexisted with, and complemented, factory production, and foreign immigrants and women have always provided a pool of cheap and largely unorganized labor.

Above

This magazine advertisement, c.1900, depicts the popular activity of cycling. However, it also hints at a dilemma for the 1900s woman — what to wear on the bicycle? Bloomers or Rational Dress were considered rather racy, and only the more daring wore them.

[1](Beaton, Cecil, *The Glass of Fashion,* Weidenfeld and Nicolson, London, 1954, p6.)

[2](As quoted by Thompson, Paul, *The Edwardians,* Weidenfeld and Nicolson, London, 1975, p20.)

[3](Veblen, Thorstein, *The Theory of the Leisure Class,* Allen & Unwin, London, 1954, p121.)

[4](Roberts, Robert, *The Classic Slum,* Manchester University Press, 1972, p11.)

Opposite page Tailor-made suits and a coat, illustrated in The Gentlewoman, 1907. Note the great variety of detailing on these garments and the women's highly decorated wide brimmed hats. All wear high collars, and muffs were also very fashionable.

Far left Decorative tailored costume in mauve and yellow for the races, with extravagant hat. **Far left** (bottom) Tailored suits, 1902. **Above** Illustration of women enjoying skating in their wide skirted suits. Hats were always worn out of doors. **Left** Beautifully detailed pale blue suit with fur muff by Paquin, 1907.

23

DAY DRESS

IM SOMMERKLEIDE   Paul Haustein (München)

Above Art Nouveau fashion drawing, 1903. Art Nouveau, very fashionable between 1890 and 1910, was an international movement within the decorative arts and architecture. This illustration was taken from the Viennese magazine Jugend.

Northern European Art Nouveau was less exuberant and made more use of rectilinear motifs than that from the South. Art Nouveau was an exclusive style, and did not filter down market.

Right Liberty silk and velvet day dress, 1905. This London department store was famous for its aesthetic dress based on classical lines, of which this is an example.

Top left These walking costumes of 1903 emphasize the fashionable S-bend and mono bosom of the period.

Bottom left Photograph of a woman wearing the characteristic blouse and skirt, c.1903.

Above Elaborate day dress with high-necked collar, 1903, illustrated with a decorative Art Nouveau border. These costumes clearly signified the wearer's wealth.

EVENING DRESS

Left Reception gown with fur wrap, 1902. Note the elaborate neckline worn with a flower, unusual shoulder straps and choker necklace. Beneath this outer splendor, the Edwardians were often quite dirty and perfumed themselves heavily to mask body odor. Hair was carefully back combed, and hair pieces often supplemented existing growth to achieve the fashionable piled effect on the top of the head.

Above Ornate evening gowns, 1902. These are heavily decorated with lace, ribbon and embroidery.
Right The wrap, designed for theater or restaurant wear, was made of faced cloth and trimmed with silk braid. It was available in ivory, biscuit, helio and pale blue. The Empire evening gown, designed for young ladies, came in white, sky, pink, mauve and black. Both are from 1907.

SPORTSWEAR AND ACCESSORIES

Above Spring hats, liberally
decorated with flowers and fruit,
and ornate blouses, 1902.

Top Heavy traveling coat, 1907.
Above left Mrs Hillyard in a long-
skirted tennis outfit, 1900. Tennis
attracted widespread female
participation from the 1870s when
women played in dresses with
bustles.

Above right The famous S-bend
corset, enforced with whalebone,
1908.

Left Richly decorated millinery and dresses, c.1905.

MEN AND CHILDREN

Left An English country gentleman, 1901. **Right** Young man dressed for sport, 1907. His functional garments are no different from those worn today — and a great contrast to the bulky clothing women were compelled to wear for modesty's sake at the same date. **Below** The fun loving King Edward VII at Windsor.

Opposite page. Left Gentleman dressed formally for the races, 1906. **Top center** Dress suit, Eton suit and Dress Carlton suits for privileged young men and boys, 1907. **Far right** (top) Naval style costumes to be made at home for children of both sexes, 1907. Note the emphasis on royal endorsement. **Bottom** Silk party dresses for young girls, 1907. The older girls are acquiring the same S-bend silhouette as their mothers.

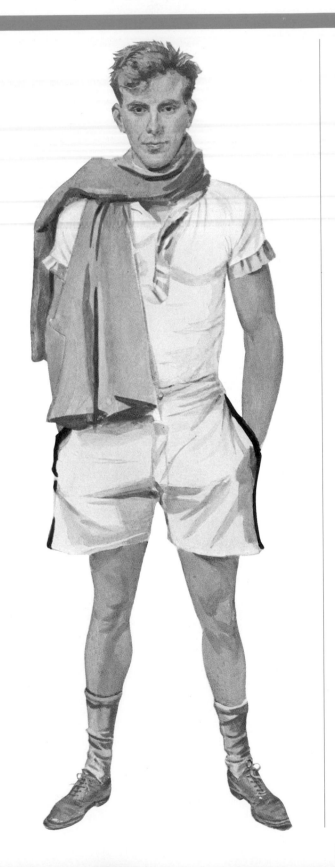

CHAPTER·TWO
1909
TO
1919

From 1908 until the advent of World War I, Paul Poiret was one of the most influential and publicized of Paris couturiers. He worked for the House of Worth and for Jacques Doucet before setting up his own couture house in 1904. Three years later he took the radical step of freeing women of fashion from corsets, although it took many of them several years to adjust, and it was not the first time. The English Rational and Aesthetic dress movements of the 1880s and 90s had abandoned corsets in the belief that women's clothing should not be restrictive, but had few followers. However, the Paris Chamber of Commerce were so alarmed about the repercussions that this change in fashion would have upon the corset industry that they sent a delegate to beg Poiret to reverse this trend, which he flatly refused to do.

In complete contrast to the styles worn during the early years of the century, Poiret dressed his daring customers in harem pantaloons and lampshade tunics, and wrapped their heads in turbans decorated with extravagant plumes. These oriental styles emerged in conjunction with the first performance of the Ballets Russes in Paris in 1909. In stark contrast to the pastel-colored scenery and traditional costumes of classical ballet, the Ballets Russes founder, Serge Diaghilev, employed Benois and Bakst to create vibrant and rich oriental designs. The results dazzled audiences and greatly influenced the decorative arts of the day. Poiret always maintained that he created his styles independently from those seen in the Russian Ballets. Cecil Beaton described him as an egocentric genius, who had no respect for good taste: "He forced his victims to wear chin straps of pearls, slung them with white foxes, stabbed them with fantastic ospreys, imprisoned them (as one hobbles the forelegs of a horse to prevent him from running away) in harem skirts. Wired tunics like lampshades were hung around the ladies' hips, heavy capes enveloped them, and they were laden with tassels and barbaric jewels."[1]

Poiret loved the rich and exotic, and his costume balls, where the guests dressed in oriental costumes or as mythological creatures, became legendary. Although his harem pantaloons were not widely adopted, oriental styles of dress and accessories were. The immensely impractical hobble skirt, which he introduced in 1913, was worn by leisured women to whom mobility was of little concern. Most women continued to wear long, narrow skirts, which were not quite so restrictive.

Poiret was a great showman and traveled round Europe with nine mannequins, publicizing his fashion. In 1914 he went on a lecture tour of the United States and was enraged to discover that replicas of his models, complete with labels, were selling in the shops for as little as $15. This sum was nonetheless too expensive for working and many middle class women. With reference to American *Vogue*, Edna Woolman Chase states that at this time, "...wanting, yet fearing, publicity the couture tried to palm off on us

LASSITUDE

Robe de dîner, de Paul Poiret

Left
Design by Paul Poiret, 1912,
illustrated by Georges Lepape.

Above
Illustration by Valentine Gross for
La Gazette du Bon Ton, 1915.
Gross also painted scenery for the
Ballets Russes. This plate, entitled
Il Pleut Encore, shows suits with
bulbous skirts by (from left to
right) Paquin, Lanvin and
Doeuillet, and a coat by Paquin.

Top right
Controversial exotic dancer and
World War I spy, Mata Hari.

Below right
This American girl, pictured in
1917, is a young war worker,
repairing army uniforms.

amateur sketches of their inferior designs instead of
allowing us to make good drawings or photographs of
their best."[2]

The Protective Association of French Dressmakers,
formed by Poiret in 1914, aimed to clamp down on this
style piracy. The *Chambre Syndicale de la Couture
Parisienne,* which dated back to 1868, also tried to do this;
but it is an inevitable consequence of couture that its
designs are copied. Poiret was an important figure not only
for his fashion designs, but also for the influence he had
upon fashion presentation and for the foundation
of a decorative arts school, the Ecole Martine, in 1912.

In 1908 Poiret commissioned a young illustrator, Paul
Iribe, to draw his costumes, which were to be reproduced
in an album. Like many fashion drawings today, they did
not accurately delineate the styles, but created a stylistic
impression. Although this album appeared in a small,
limited edition, it greatly publicized his couture house and
in 1911 he employed Georges Lepape to produce another.
The style of these illustrations reached a wider audience,
although still a minority, through *La Gazette du Bon Ton,*
founded in 1912. This exclusive magazine, published

quarterly on handmade paper with hand colored plates, reflected mainstream art movements. The heavily stylistic drawings of regular contributors Iribe, Lepape, Georges Barbier, Valentine Gross and Charles Marty introduced a fresh and influential approach to portraying fashion. In 1925, *La Gazette du Bon Ton* merged with *Vogue*.

The work of the Ecole Martine gained an international reputation during these years. Poiret sought out 12-year-old working class girls who had left school but had no formal art training or preconceived ideas about drawing, and paid them a wage to work at the Martine. He took these girls to parks and zoos and told them to draw whatever they saw. He then applied their magical and naive images to designs for carpets (which they made themselves), furnishings, wallpapers, ceramics and wall murals. He also used their images for textile and embroidery designs. An exhibition of their work was held at the important Salon d'Automne in 1912.

Mariano Fortuny was another highly creative designer of the period. Born in Spain, Fortuny lived in Venice and was entirely self-taught. He was a talented painter and primarily saw himself as an artist rather than a dressmaker. Fortuny's garments were timeless: their design hardly changed during his working life, from 1900-1949, and as a result he rarely appeared in the fashion magazines of the period. His clothing had a renaissance elegance and often used classical draping; and the fabric designs were greatly influenced by those from the fifteenth and sixteenth centuries. He may have been influenced by the Pre-Raphaelite paintings of Rosetti and Burne-Jones, which portrayed women wearing renaissance styles of clothing. Fortuny, who had studied mechanics and chemistry, had his own secret methods of printing and embossing fabric so that they resembled ancient brocades. He tended to use faded-looking rich colors and often worked with gold and silver threads. In the tradition of William Morris, he believed that the designer and maker should be one.

His most famous garments were his Delphos dresses. To prevent these pleated sheaths from being copied he took out a patent on their design in 1909. The fabric for these dresses was so light that their hems had to be weighted with tiny metal beads. When they were not being worn they could be stored tied in a knot, and miraculously retained their pleats.

During World War I, daytime dress was dominated by uniforms and utilitarian wear. The sudden demand for female labor occasioned by the war drew an additional 1.7 million women into the labor force in Great Britain alone. Before 1914, women in the West represented approximately one-third of the total labor force, and married women represented just one-tenth of these. This was, however, the first time that many middle and upper class women had ever earned a living, let alone performed routine factory jobs or heavy farm work. Women munitions

workers wore trousers and overalls, and nurses and ambulance drivers wore uniforms. Most women dressed in ankle-length skirts, wide at the bottom, with loose jackets tied in the middle with a broad belt. Although materials were hard to obtain and labor scarce, many of the couture houses remained open during the hostilities. In 1915, the international San Francisco exhibition provided an outlet for the Paris couturiers to display their models to an American audience.

Poiret refused to surrender to the economies necessitated by the war and continued to create extravagant garments such as shortened crinoline styles with pagoda hips. Fashion responded gradually to wartime changes in society but these did not reach a peak until the mid 1920s; since Poiret did not fit in with these changes, his popularity died.

[1](Beaton, Cecil *The Glass of Fashion*, Weidenfeld and Nicolson, London, 1954, p17.)
[2](Already cited. p98)

Above

Suffragettes, c.1910. Organized campaigns for women's suffrage had existed in Britain since 1865, but only hit the headlines when the Women's Social and Political Union decided to take militant action in 1906, with suffragette women deliberately courting arrest. Militancy was stepped up in 1909, with campaigns of organized vandalism — window breaking, arson — and hunger striking on imprisonment.

PREWAR DAY DRESS

LES DESSOUS
A
LA MODE

LA mode actuelle impose des dessous légers.

Sur la chemise courte, en fin tissu de soie, une combinaison de soie également, à mailles serrées. Chemise et combinaisons ne sont retenues sur l'épaule que par des faveurs étroites.

C'est chez Lemaître, qu'il convient de choisir ces frivolités. Il vend aussi les seuls bas de soie élégants.

Left *Fashionable outfit trimmed with fox fur, 1913.*

Above *Fashion drawings for underwear by Marty, for La Gazette du Bon Ton, 1912. This shows the choice of summer and winter underwear.*

Left Visiting robe by Paquin, drawn by Barbier for La Gazette du Bon Ton, *1912. Note the Art Deco-style fabric.* **Above** Costume worn at Longchamp Races, 1910. The cut and draped detailing on the dress accentuated the woman's fashionable hourglass figure.

COATS AND SUITS

Below *Studio photograph of a woman wearing a fashionable but cheap (note the rough hemlines and stitching) suit, c.1912.* **Right** *Burberry coat, 1917. Burberry and Aquascutum were the leading makers of protective outer coats for men and women. Their garments were widely worn for motoring.* **Far right** *Women wearing expensive fur coats, 1914.*

Left Woman wearing a heavily embroidered and fringed evening coat, 1909; it is a good example of the very elaborate clothing that the rich wore during the early years of the twentieth century. **Below** Studio photograph of a woman wearing a typical, wide belted suit with a three-quarter length jacket, 1915.

EVENING DRESS

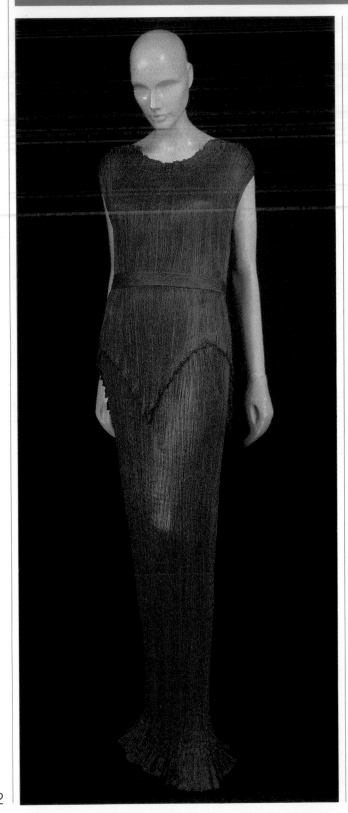

L'ADIEU DANS LA NUIT

Robe du soir de Paquin

Left *Fortuny's pleated sheath Delphos dress, 1912. The intricacy of this garment clearly could not be translated for the mass market.*

Above *Elaborate, oriental evening dress designed by Paquin, 1913, and drawn by Marty for* La Gazette du Bon Ton *— another style reserved for the rich.*

Above *Evening robe by Talbot of Paris, 1913. Note the oriental head-dress.*

Right *Evening gown by the English dressmaking establishment, Jays Ltd, 1908. The exquisite hand embroidery must have taken hundreds of hours to work.*

WARTIME CLOTHING

Top left Women serving in the Land Army being presented to the Queen. Their practical uniforms consisted of coats, knee breeches and leggings. **Far left** (bottom) Snapshot, 1919. Note the young boys' Norfolk jackets, knee length shorts and black wool stockings. **Middle** (bottom) This relatively functional and comfortable style of dress was widely worn by women during the war. **Below** Snapshot, 1916. Typical of clothing widely worn by women during the period, the older woman's clothes seem almost Victorian, whilst the younger woman wears a casual style which looks ahead to the 1920s. **Right** American magazine advertisement, 1914-1915 **Far right** Woman's suit, 1919, with shortened skirt and spats.

THE very newest style is portrayed in this elegant garment. The material used is an all silk satin which will be extremely popular this fall and winter. A most stunning and easily becoming style. The bodice of dress is made in semi-fitting modified basque effect shirred in front. Cuffs and standing collar of fine quality organdy, trimmed with silk embroidered paon velvet which makes a very handsome trimming. Waist in back extends slightly below girdle in coatee effect and is trimmed with self covered buttons. Underwaist is lace trimmed. Handsome plaited Russian tunic skirt. Dress fastens in front. A dress that is popular both for afternoon and evening wear. Women's sizes only. Give measurements. Avg. shpg. wt., 2¼ lbs.

No. 31A4465½
Amethyst.

No. 31A4466½
Russian green.

No. 31A4467½
Black.
Price,
each.................$19.95

SIZES—These Dresses will be furnished in the following sizes only: From 32 up to and including 44 inches bust measure; waist measure up to and including 33 inches, and front skirt length, of 39 or 42 inches, with wide basted hem. See page 499 for simple measuring instructions.

THE all wool English gabardine cloth used in making up this 1915 advanced model is greatly in demand this season. This garment has wonderful style. It has been copied from a very expensive model and makes a serviceable and rich looking dress. The vestee, round collar and cuffs are made of good quality satin. Yoke and collar are of Oriental top embroidered net, collar being wired to stand up. Loose hanging waist in coatee or jacket effect, high waisted and button trimmed both front and back. Long flaring Russian tunic skirt, with fine quality silk satin flounce on underskirt. Dress closes invisibly in front. Women's sizes only. Give measurements. Average shipping weight, 2½ pounds.

No. 31A4460½
Navy blue; black satin bottom.

No. 31A4461½
Navy blue; navy blue satin bottom.
Price,
each.................$16.50

SIZES—These Dresses will be furnished in the following sizes only: From 32 up to and including 44 inches bust measure; waist measure up to and including 33 inches, and front skirt length of 39 or 42 inches, with wide basted hem. See page 499 for simple measuring instructions.

Sears, Roebuck and Co., Chicago, Ill.

The cover of a sheet music collection of songs from the 1920s musical Wonder Bar.

CHAPTER·THREE
1920
TO
1929

In the post-war years, the idea that a woman would give up "gainful" employment upon marriage continued to be accepted, with the exception of the very poor. Women did, however, enjoy a greater variety of leisure activities outside of the home, the most significant of which was the growth of paid annual holidays, often spent at seaside resorts; and on a more regular basis, public dancing, taboo in Victorian times, became immensely popular among all classes.

Art Deco — influenced by Egyptian and African art, Cubism, Fauvism, Expressionism and European Purism — was the dominant decorative style of the 1920s and 30s. The 1925 Paris *Exposition des Arts Décoratifs et Industriels Modernes* acted as a showcase for this movement, which embraced the Modern Age and largely rejected historical reference. The first decorative style which did not remain exclusive, and seized upon by manufacturers, Art Deco's abstract and geometrical motifs were liberally applied to a vast range of goods, from garden gates to cosmetic compacts, and greatly influenced textile design. Avidly consumed by the fashion hungry postwar market, dress also became widely available in the form of readymade clothes; but although many women wore garments of a similar design, the wealth of the wearer was only slightly less obvious than in prewar years. Social status continued to be indicated by sartorial superiority and the two remained inextricably entwined.

The fashions of the 1920s were dominated by what became known as the "Garçonne Look," which had reached its peak by 1926. Cecil Beaton describes how the fashion illustrators drew "... those longer than life ladies who, with their short, tubular dresses, cigarettes in long holders, cloche hats, bobbed hair, plucked eyebrows, bands of diamond bracelets from wrist to elbow and earrings hanging like fuchsias symbolized the visual aspect of the period."[1] As its name suggests, the "Garçonne Look" was boyish in comparison with the accentuated feminine curves so desirable in previous decades. Hemlines had crept up from the beginning of the 1920s to reach just above the knee in 1926. Never before had a woman revealed so much of her legs. In contrast, waistlines dropped from their natural position to the hips.

It was the Parisian couturiers Gabrielle Chanel and Jean Patou who were largely responsible for creating this dramatic new style. They recognized that the post-war women would no longer accept being immobilized and contorted into unnatural shapes in the name of fashion. Although for some the new styles involved dieting, wearing breast-flattening bras and narrow, elastic, boneless corsets, these were relatively light concessions to make in comparison to the constriction of Edwardian profiles. Chanel and Patou dressed the modern woman in loose fitting, comfortable and functional garments, many of which were based along the lines of sportswear and the

Above
Noel Coward pictured at home in 1927. Note the Art Deco headboard and bedspread.

Left
Film star Clara Bow was dubbed the "It" Girl by popular novelist Elinor Glynn.

clothing of working people. Indeed, they were often credited with creating a *poverty-de-luxe.*

The couture industry had traditionally used the finest and most expensive silks for its garments. Chanel therefore created quite a furore when she introduced what had always been regarded as rather humble fabrics — such as knitted jersey — in simply cut suits and dresses for society women, while still designing the most luxurious bead-encrusted evening dresses and trenchcoats with sable

linings. Chanel was only too delighted when her clothing was widely copied, aware that the quality and cut of the original would always stand out. She promoted an understated elegance, believing that women rather than their clothing should be highlighted. Indeed, her own appearance epitomized the fashions she created. The perfume Chanel No 5 was introduced in 1921 and from that date onwards its sales helped to support the house of Chanel. Patou designed styles akin to those of Chanel, and the two remained great rivals throughout the 1920s. Wealthy, fashion conscious men of the period sported Oxford bags, Fair Isle jumpers (as popularized by the Prince of Wales), plus fours and two tone shoes.

The "Roaring Twenties" automatically conjures up images of these "Bright Young Things" clad in their adventurous clothing, sipping cocktails and dancing the Charleston until the early hours. While this exhilarating experience was enjoyed by a few, hunger marches and longterm unemployment were the stark reality for a great many people. In between these polarized socio-economic extremes there existed a large section of the population in Britain and the United States who experienced a decrease in the cost of living and an increase in real earnings. This group formed the mass market for women's fashionable ready-to-wear clothing, which became available during this decade.

For the first time, the essence of couture could be adapted and translated for mass production. The small quantity of fabric required for, and, the simplicity of, the loose fitting fashionable tubular shapes enabled manufacturers to copy the styles of high fashion. Ultimately, they were suitable for the lifestyle of working women and housewives as well as the patrons of couture.

The introduction of rayon was, in design and manufacturing terms, one of the most significant textile developments of the twentieth century and was a great boon to the production of ready-to-wear clothes. Attempts had been made to perfect a synthetic fiber since the 1880s, but these had met with little success. In the immediate postwar years rayon (or artificial silk as it was known before 1926) was used to line the cheaper ranges of menswear. Its breakthrough, however, lay in the manufacture of stockings, the demand for which was stimulated by the fashion for shorter skirts. Rayon stockings ran easily, but they cost a quarter of the price of silk ones. Women sometimes wore them inside out and powdered their legs to subdue the shine. Dyeing and production methods were improved during the late 1920s and rayon became increasingly used as dress fabric. As it superficially resembled the feel and appearance of natural silk, rayon enabled manufacturers to emulate top quality knitwear and silk garments at a fraction of the cost.

In spite of the availability of ready-made fashions, most working and many middle class women made a great deal of their own, and their children's, clothing at home. This was for financial reasons and, for a proficient dressmaker, to obtain individual and perfectly fitting garments. Down market fashion magazines — such as *Mab's* in Great Britain — illustrated fashionable garments which could be made at home and often included a free paper pattern. In the United States, where many families lived a considerable distance from the nearest town, such magazines and mail-order catalogs — of which Sears Roebuck was among the

largest — were invaluable for keeping in touch with the latest trends.

In 1929 the hemline dropped, the waistline returned to its natural position and the bosom was emphasized once more, these realignments signaling a change to the more figure molding styles of the 1930s. In 1929, the 20s came to a dramatic climax when the American Stock Exchange collapsed with devastating financial repercussions around the world.

[1](Beaton, Cecil, *The Glass of Fashion,* Weidenfeld & Nicolson, London, 1954, p133.)

Above

Funeral procession for Emmeline Pankhurst. Mrs Pankhurst died at the age of 69 in 1928 — the year that women were given the vote on an equal footing with men — having actively campaigned for women's suffrage since 1903.

Right
The discovery of Tutankhamen's tomb in 1923 popularized the use of Egyptian motifs in all branches of the decorative arts and formed a considerable part of the Art Deco style.

DAY DRESS

LA BAGUE NEUVE
OU
LA JALOUSIE DISSIMULÉE

ROBES. DE PAUL POIRET

Far left *Fashionable woman at Ascot, 1925.* **Above left** *Egyptian inspired dress by Vionnet, after the opening of Tutankhamen's tomb, c.1922.* **Left** *Snapshot, c.1928. Note how similar the women's dress and shoe designs are. Fashion during the 20s was much more rigid than it is today.* **Above** *These dresses of 1924 are among Poiret's most simple designs.*

Unusual Values

Stylish Dresses at Moderate Prices

16 X 220
Crepe
$4⁹⁸

16 X 225
Embroidered
"Hard Twist"
Voile
$8⁹⁸

16 X 221
Embroidered
Voile
$5⁹⁸

22 X 3091
Hand-
Embroidered
Voile
$2⁷⁹

16 X 223
Pure
Linen
$7⁴⁹

16 X 224
Imported
Ratine
$6⁹⁸

16 X 222
Figured
Crepe
$2⁹⁸

Left American ready-to-wear, medium-priced dresses of 1924.

Below Photographs of a fashionable woman, c. 1926. By this date the design of women's dress was simple and often based on sportswear.

53

Left Photograph of Sir Winston Churchill, 1927.
Bottom left Snapshot showing women wearing fur coats with big collars and cloche hats, c. 1926. Around this date, cloches were worn deep over the brow. **Right** Tailored suit by Beer, 1922. The waisted jacket is reminiscent of the Edwardian era and the shorter skirt of the 1920s.
Above The couturier Chanel, 1928, wearing one of her classic, understated outfits.

EVENING DRESS

Far left Evening dress, c.1926. During the 20s it was often only the use of richer fabrics and decorative detailing which differentiated day from evening dress. **Above** A fashion drawing of elegant evening dresses with trains, pictured in a classical setting, House of Worth, 1924. Illustration, La Gazette du Bon Ton. **Left** Dress by Jeanne Lanvin, worn with an ornate bandeau around the hips, c.1928.

Right Evening dress with plunging backline and uneven hem, 1924. Uneven hemlines appear where there is uncertainty as to whether the hem will rise or fall. Illustration, La Gazette du Bon Ton. **Far right** Beaded evening dress, c.1926. These beads were individually applied with a tambour hook, and such dresses often weighed up to 9lbs. This weight helped them to hang in the fashionable straight style from the shoulders.

SPORTSWEAR AND ACCESSORIES

Above Beachwear drawn by René Vincent, 1927. **Left** Bathing, 1926. This style of bathing suit, made of wool or cotton, was worn by men, women and children throughout the 1920s. Never before had women exposed so much of their bodies in public and never before had they been able to swim unencumbered by bulky swimming costumes.

Above Chemise c. 1926. By the 1920s most women did not wear corsets, although some bound their hips and wore breast flattening bras to achieve the fashionable boyish figure. Chemises like this one were widely worn throughout the decade.

Above Women's Golf outfit. Jeanne Lanvin, 1925. Drawn by George Lepape for La Gazette du Bon Ton. During the 1920s women enjoyed a greater variety of sports activities than ever before. By this date there was little difference between the design of sports and everyday dress. **Top right** Bathing costumes and beach pajamas, 1928. Beach pajamas were the only trousers which most women wore during the 1920s.

Right Susanne Lenglen, the French tennis champion, c. 1922. Lenglen, who was dressed by Patou, personified the 1920s "New Woman." Her sleeveless tennis dresses were worn daringly short, revealing the top of her stockings.

MEN AND CHILDREN

Left These 1927 drawings of coat styles for young girls aged 4-10 years reveal how similar their design was to womenswear.
Bottom left This photograph, c.1923, represents the plain style of suits that most men wore. **Below** Photograph of two young girls, c.1924, the one on the left wearing a knitted dress and the other a velvet one.

Above The Prince of Wales wearing a Fair Isle sweater, c.1925. Many men, copying the royal example, adopted these sweaters during the 1920s.

DANSONS LA CAPUCINE

ROBE D'ÉTÉ ET ROBES D'ENFANTS, DE JEANNE LANVIN

Gazette du Bon Ton.   *Année 1921.* —

" J'AI FAILLI ATTENDRE "

COSTUME VESTON. DE LUS ET BEFVE

Année 1922. — Planche

Left *Illustration of children's dresses by Jeanne Lanvin, 1921. Pierre Brissaud for La Gazette du Bon Ton.* **Above** *Fashionable man wearing double-breasted suit, 1922. Rejelan for La Gazette du Bon Ton.* **Right** *Heartthrob film star Ronald Colman, c.1928.*

HAIR, HATS AND ACCESSORIES

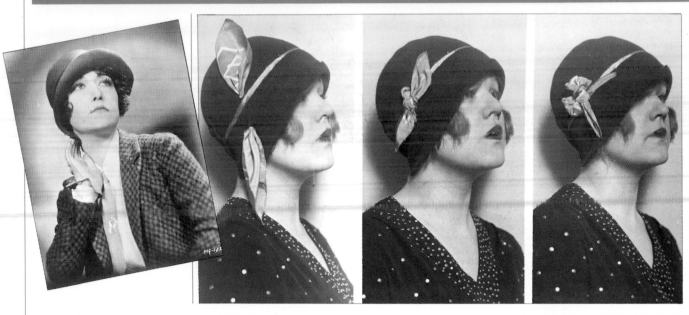

Far left (top) Film star Dorothy Sebastian wearing rolled felt cloche hat, c.1926. **Left** Taken from an unspecified newspaper, the caption to these photographs describes the "love symbol" hats: "By varying the position of the ribbon, the wearer signifies her status as regards matrimony. When she wears it 'arrow-like'...she is single, but her promise has been given. Tied in a bow [center] she is married. The arrangement on the right signifies single blessedness, widowed or divorced, which is to say "fancy free." Now the young man has but to study the symbols of the hat to discover where he stands." **Far left** (bottom) Jean Grangier illustration of shoes for La Gazette du Bon Ton, 1924. **Bottom left** Film star Anita Page wearing pale blue cloche hat c.1926.

Right Art Deco-style evening purse studded with diamanté, and with lipstick concealed in the tassles, c.1925. **Far right** Fashion illustration of Camille Roger's wide-brimmed hats for La Gazette du Bon Ton, 1921.

Evening dress c.1932.

CHAPTER·FOUR

1930
TO
1939

Throughout the Depression, the luxury trades in Paris — supported by the French government — remained intact. The couture industry did, however, lose much of its lucrative export trade in its fall in sales to the United States. As a result, many houses introduced top quality ready-to-wear lines to supplement their continuing sales of individually made items; there remained a body of rich patrons who were either unaffected by, or who had profited from, the economic crises.

Fashion in the 1930s rejected the angular severity of the previous decade and replaced it with a sleek, streamlined look, achieved by bias cutting of materials and the use of smooth fabrics. The new silhouette, which followed the line of the figure, closely hugged the waist and hips and then fell into a soft, flared skirt. Daytime hemlines reached midcalf length and often dropped to the ankle for evening wear. In contrast to the rather uniform styles of the 1920s, fashion during the 30s succumbed to many influences, all of which shared an element of escapism and fantasy.

During this decade the Parisian couturiers Madeleine Vionnet and Madame Grés became famous for their intricately bias cut and pleated dresses. Madame Grés, who worked under the name of Alix during the 1930s, had a passion for classical sculpture and sought to recapture some of its timeless elegance in her clothing. The fluid garments that these two women created were invariably photographed in a neo-classical setting; themes from Greek legends, classically draped figures and pillars were used as backdrops for the statuesque models who displayed these garments. Paris based Hoyningen Heune was one of the leading fashion photographers who worked in this vein.

The surreal art movement also exerted some influence on fashions during the 1930s. In 1936 — 10 years after the surrealist manifesto was written — the first exhibition of surrealism was held in England, at Burlington House. This attracted some 20,000 people and enticed even larger audiences when it transferred to New York afterward. Fashion illustrators for *Vogue* — such as Christian Berard — adopted the style of surrealism and drew women carrying their heads under their arms. Horst photographed models coiled in rope, which hurtled into oblivion, or posed next to cracked mirrors. With the exception of the Parisian couturier Elsa Schiaparelli, surrealism showed its influence upon the presentation of fashion, rather than upon garment design. Many of the more decorative aspects of the movement filtered down market, as it was easy to copy the imagery without understanding the ideology.

Schiaparelli loved the bizarre and turned to the artists of surrealism — and particularly Salvador Dali — to assist her in her search for novelty. Schiaparelli dressed Dali's wife free of charge and he in turn provided the inspiration for many of her designs. Dali dyed an enormous stuffed bear shocking pink (the name and use of the color was

Schiaparelli's trademark), put drawers in its stomach, and then dressed it in an orchid-colored satin jacket and adorned it with jewels for her salon.

Many of her designs were outrageously daring, such as the 1936 black hat shaped like a shoe with shocking pink heel which Mrs Reginald Fellowes had the courage to wear. Another hat, which Schiaparelli herself wore, resembled a lamb cutlet with a frill on the bone. Even her classically draped evening dresses were decorated with the most unusual motifs — such as a large red lobster splattered across the front — and she was also famous for her unusual accessories (bags which looked like bird cages, buttons in the shapes of lips and lollipops, and the use of zippers on couture garments). But even though Schiaparelli dressed the most adventurous society women of this period, she also had a large conservative clientele, for whom she designed more subdued classical garments.

Throughout the 1930s the clothing worn by Hollywood's stars provided a major new fashion focus. Joan Crawford, Greta Garbo, Ginger Rogers, Marlene Dietrich and Jean Harlow were among the many glamorous actresses whose hairstyles, make-up and clothing were avidly copied by European and American women. The

Above
Jeanne Lanvin's Surreal haute couture display for the 1937 Paris Exhibition.

Right
Joan Crawford in lounging pyjamas.

Far right
Adrian's design for the film Letty Lynton, *worn here by Joan Crawford in the title role, 1932.*

actresses received much greater exposure than the mannequins on the catwalks of Paris. Each week some twenty million people in Great Britain and eighty-five million in the United States packed the movie houses to soak up the escapist world of Hollywood.

During the 1920s, Hollywood aimed to dress the stars in the very latest styles, and sent scores of stylists to Paris to keep them informed of fashion changes. On occasion, the studios commissioned the great dictators of style to design garments for the films, but the crunch came in 1929, when thousands of feet of film were discarded because Patou had

unexpectedly lowered his hemline, and this footage had been shot showing garments with shorter lengths. In an attempt to overcome such problems the studios began to promote the talents of their own designers, such as Adrian, Travis Banton, Walter Plunkett and Edith Head. Although their designs varied little from those created in Paris, the studio designers made their garments more elaborate. The fashion elite often condemned the stars for being too "showy," but to many of the less well off fashion hungry

Above
Vivien Leigh as Scarlett O'Hara in Gone with the Wind, *1939.*

women who worked long hours in dull jobs they represented the ultimate in style and beauty.

The stars did become associated with, and promote, certain styles, such as Greta Garbo's trenchcoats and berets, and perhaps the most famous example of all, the dress with large ruffled sleeves which Adrian designed for Joan Crawford to wear as Letty Lynton in the film of the same name (1932). This has frequently been credited with instigating the fashion for padded shoulders, although Schiaparelli and Marcel Rochas had included them in their collections the previous year. It was not, however, until a Hollywood star wore them in a screen hit that they became widely adopted and invariably associated with this actress. In spite of the fact that *Letty Lynton* was withdrawn soon after general release (as a result of a copyright infringement), Macy's in New York is reputed to have sold over 500,000 copies of this dress. Many department stores had "Cinema Departments," which sold reproductions of garments from specific films at low prices, and fan magazines — such as *Filmfair* in Great Britain and *Photoplay* in the United States — further promoted the styles worn by the queens of Hollywood.

Male stars provided their own contemporary wardrobes and just had to ensure that their clothing was in harmony with that worn by the leading lady. The double-breasted suits with wide lapels and cuffs on the trousers which Robert Taylor, Clark Gable, Spencer Tracy and Tyrone Power wore were widely copied by the male audience, as were their mannerisms, mustaches and hairstyles.

During the interwar years fashion went full circle. In great contrast to the "Garçonne Look," by the mid-1930s Norman Hartnell was designing evening dresses in Great Britain inspired by the painter Winterhalter, for Queen Elizabeth II among many patrons. Winterhalter was famous for his portraits of aristocratic and society women — notably for the painting of the Empress Eugénie and ladies of the court *c.*1860. Balenciaga and Vionnet also featured this type of dress between 1937-1939. Only the wealthiest women could ultimately afford and enjoy a social life which made wearing a crinoline possible and they were often seen at debutante balls. These crinolines were made in whalebone instead of steel. Alternatively, a similar effect was obtained by sewing whalebone hoops into a detachable skirt, or even by using stiff horse hair and taffeta petticoats under a very full skirt. In keeping with this romantic revival, many designers added a bustle to the back of their dresses, while this vogue for Victoriana was also witnessed in interior design and the literature of the period.

On September 3, 1939 war in Europe was declared. For the next seven years a wartime style of dress was created and fashion remained static until Christian Dior presented his Corole line in 1947, evolved from these fashions created before the World War II.

DRESSES AND SUITS

Models—
AUGUSTA BERNARD

The delightful beige suit above has a very new story to tell—it is the line, which shows fullness in the skirt at the back, and an almost straight front.

Note, too, the brown scarf looped into a bow. The careless-looking cravat bow in a contrasting colour is the vogue with suits, as is also shown in the navy costume of woollen bouclé. The jacket of this last model is cut rather on the waisted lines of the suits in the "naughty 'nineties." So, too, is the street frock on the right of black marocain, with the short full basque at the back, and green cravat tie.

47

Left The original caption to this picture, taken in 1933, stated: "The latest Marlene Dietrich fashion has crossed the Atlantic. A mannequin appeared at a dress show this week wearing a perfectly tailored man's lounge suit and it looks as if an attempt is being made to popularize this Hollywood craze in this country." Suit from Harvey Nichols of Regent Street, London.

Above Tailored suits featured in Woman's Journal, 1932.

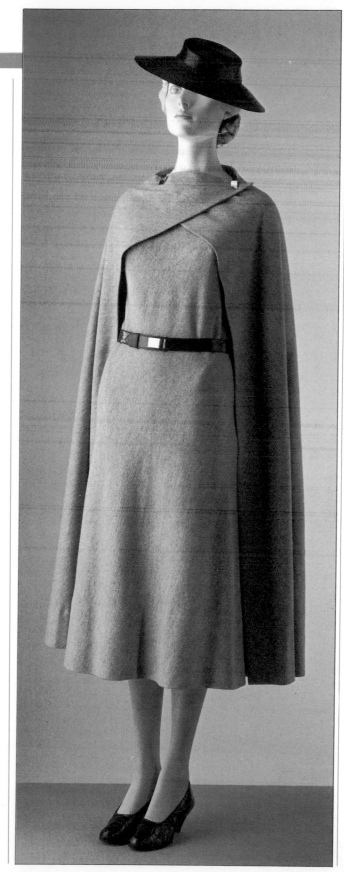

Above Coat and suit, 1935. Both of these women are wearing sailor-style straw hats at a jaunty angle.

Right Classical and beautifully-cut Vionnet suit, 1933.

EVENING DRESS

The Interest Begins at the Top!

In this charming dinner frock of satin and lace, it is the amusing and attractive sleeves which lift it to stardom. The next frock is of the same *genre* with a contrasting top, and uncommon sleeves, but it makes its contrast with pink ninon and Seville blue chiffon. Very delightful is the evening frock—its back view shows the low cartridge pleating on either side of the skirt, and the front shows the careless cowl bodice and fascinating little taffetas coatee which accompanies the model.

Muslin models cut in Paris, as well as hand-cut paper patterns are obtainable of these designs. For particulars see page 106.

Opposite page. Left Satin dress by Charles James, 1934, and fur coat by Vionnet c.1936. **Center** Evening dress called "Tears" by Schiaparelli, 1938. **Left** Striking Chanel evening dress, 1937.

Left Feature on evening dresses, Women's Journal, 1932. This middle market magazine is displaying fashionable garments which readers can make from paper patterns. Note the emphasis on muslin models "cut in Paris." **Above** Evening outfit by French couturier Nina Ricci, 1937.

MEN AND CHILDREN

Below Men wearing boater hats, 1934. **Bottom** The Duke of Windsor, then Prince of Wales, with his brother, Prince George, 1931. **Right** Working men at a fishing port, 1936.

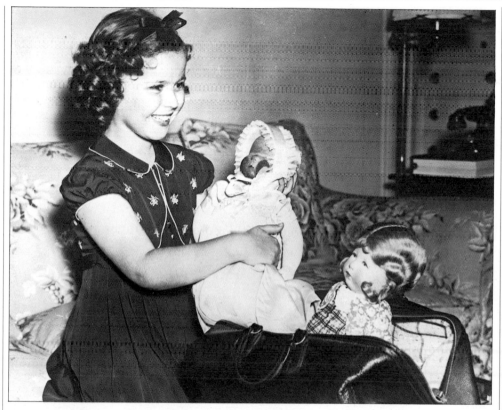

Far left (top) Shirley Temple, c.1934, exerted a great influence upon children's dress and hairstyles. **Far left** (bottom) A poor mining community, 1935. **Left** Young girl in Shirley Temple style dress and curls. **Below** Young girl with pram, 1933.

75

BEACHWEAR AND UNDERWEAR

Above These women, wearing beach trousers over swimming costumes and trousers with halter neck fronts and straps at the back, are from c.1935. During the 1930s swimming costumes became tighter and more revealing, and in 1935 two-piece suits were shown on Vogue's pages for the first time, although they were not worn until the 1940s. **Right** Carefree models walking along the promenade, c.1935.

Left Tailored navy linen beach suit with large patch pockets and striped shorts, suit from c.1937.

Right *Girl wearing shorts at an outdoor public swimming pool.* **Below** *This pair of cami-knickers was made in Courtaulds' printed rayon crepe, 1938.*

Above *Night- and underwear as shown in the Woman's Journal, 1932.* **Left** *This photograph shows typical 1930s stockings and shoes.*

HAIR, HATS AND ACCESSORIES

Left and **below** These two hats designed for Ascot 1939 by top society milliner Aage Thaarup show the extreme variety of shape that could be worn in any one particular season.

Below A Victor Stiebel design of 1939, perched forward on the head, with the very popular veil.
Bottom Contrasting wide brimmed and pillbox straw hats as worn at Newbury Races, 1939.

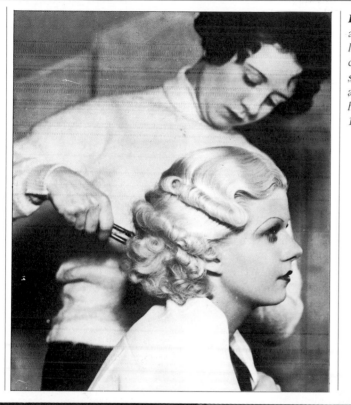

Left Thousands of women aspiring to Hollywood glamor at a low cost bleached their hair with cheap peroxides to imitate screen stars like Jean Harlow, the archetypal platinum blonde, seen here in an MGM publicity photo of 1933.

Shoes for the Cruise from the World's most beautiful Shoe Store

In the minds of Smart Women the NEW DOLCIS SUPER SHOE STORE has in one month become the Rendezvous of Fashion lovers. Its visitors . . . and there have been thousands . . . have marvelled at a new conception, fulfilled at a Shoe Store so different, so beautiful, so spacious . . . at such bewildering variety of graceful shoes.

Have you been to the American Floor in this New Dolcis Store? . . . If not, do come soon and see the "New System" American Shoes, so brilliantly designed, so versatile as to fittings, so wonderfully flexible . . . those shoes which have made American women noted for their impeccable footwear.

Or, if you wish to choose from a wealth of delicate models from the Continent . . . or from a host of Dolcis British Models . . . so well known not only for style but for their inbuilt integrity, come and select the smartest and best shoes that money can buy, from as little as 16/9, or up to four guineas . . . values unrivalled anywhere in Great Britain or the World.

DOLCIS
the world's most complete shoe store
OXFORD STREET *(facing Bond Street)*
There are parking facilities adjoining the Dolcis Store

Here are four Models selected by the Dolcis Stylist from the collection of Cruising and Summer Evening Shoes specially designed and modern New York for DOLCIS.

Also obtainable at the New Dolcis Super Shoe Store now open in Brompton Road, Knightsbridge.

Left These four models at a hairdressing fair of 1932 demonstrate the popularity of softly waved hair in the 1930s. This was a reaction to the severe bobs, crops and shingles that had seemed so daring in the 1920s.

Above This magazine advertisement of 1936 for Dolcis shoes shows feminine, strappy styles and hints at luxurious living and cruise liner trips — a popular setting for Hollywood films.

Christian Dior's "New Look" suit, 1947.

CHAPTER·FIVE
1940
TO
1949

During World War II many of the Paris couture houses remained open. Madame Grés infuriated the Germans by designing her first collection under Occupation in the colors of the French flag — and as a result of this defiance was closed for one year. But the couturiers remained open to clothe a small Franco-German set who enjoyed a glittering social life and luxurious couture clothing, existing alongside the devastating poverty that most French people suffered. There were also a few wealthy Frenchwomen who glided through the period dressing and living according to prewar standards, as if oblivious to the hostilities.

Great Britain and the United States, cut off from Paris until October 1944, had to rely upon the talents of their own designers to create wartime dress. In Britain there emerged a wartime socialism which promoted the belief that what few resources there were should be evenly distributed among the population. Clothing was put on a points system and weighted according to the quantity of fabric used and the amount of labour involved in its production. The famous *CC41* (civilian clothing 1941) utility label was introduced and became recognized as a guarantee of quality. This stylishly cut clothing was designed by the Incorporated Society of London Fashion Designers, whose members included Digby Morton, Norman Hartnell and Victor Stiebel, with the leading British couturiers conforming to a strict design brief imposed by the government. This stressed that a minimum quantity of fabric should be used and that there should be no unnecessary decorative detailing. In response to these economical requirements, hemlines were raised to just below the knee, waists were nipped-in and collars, belts and lapels, if used, were small. As silk stockings were banned, ankle socks became widely worn, and snoods, turbans and head-scarves became very popular, although hats were not rationed. Elaborately waved hairstyles and the use of facial cosmetics were highlighted to compensate for the rather austere clothing designs.

As the design of women's clothing was restricted during the utility period, manufacturers were encouraged to experiment with large-scale production. The Eastman cutter, for example, enabled a hundred or more garments to be graded and cut in one lay, which greatly increased the production process.

Initially 20 coupons were allocated to each person bi-annually — and a woman's coat alone consumed 14 of these. As the war progressed this allowance was reduced and reached its lowest level in the acute economic crisis which Britain experienced after the war. To supplement this meager allowance women were encouraged to "Make do and Mend," which became the Board of Trade's wartime slogan. The women's press provided advice on how to remake old clothing, unravel discarded sweaters and reknit new ones, and make patchwork items out of scraps of

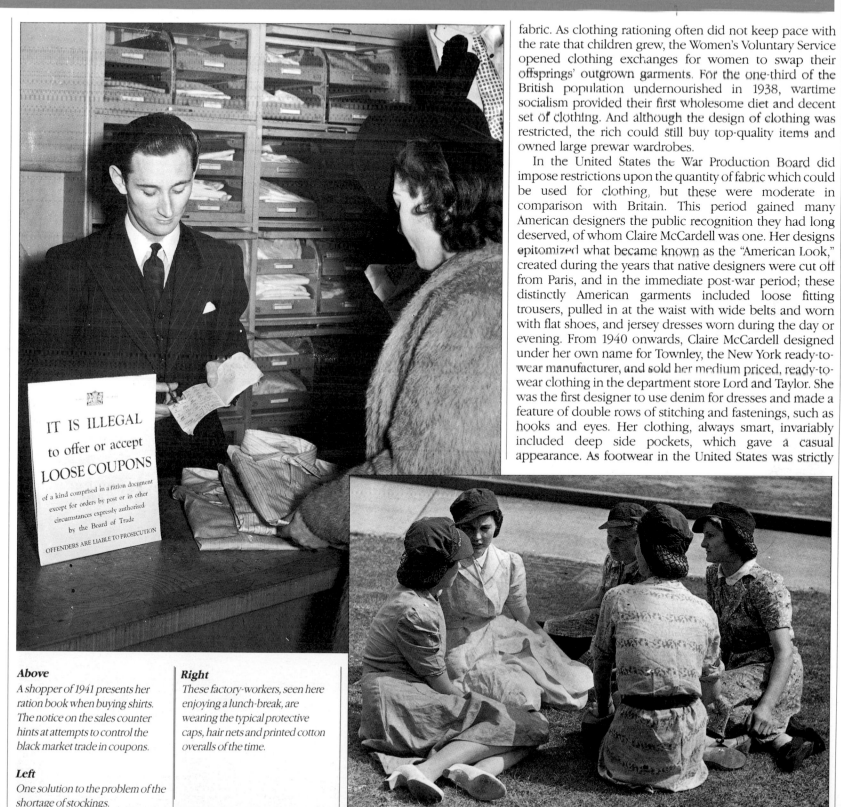

fabric. As clothing rationing often did not keep pace with the rate that children grew, the Women's Voluntary Service opened clothing exchanges for women to swap their offsprings' outgrown garments. For the one-third of the British population undernourished in 1938, wartime socialism provided their first wholesome diet and decent set of clothing. And although the design of clothing was restricted, the rich could still buy top-quality items and owned large prewar wardrobes.

In the United States the War Production Board did impose restrictions upon the quantity of fabric which could be used for clothing, but these were moderate in comparison with Britain. This period gained many American designers the public recognition they had long deserved, of whom Claire McCardell was one. Her designs epitomized what became known as the "American Look," created during the years that native designers were cut off from Paris, and in the immediate post-war period; these distinctly American garments included loose fitting trousers, pulled in at the waist with wide belts and worn with flat shoes, and jersey dresses worn during the day or evening. From 1940 onwards, Claire McCardell designed under her own name for Townley, the New York ready-to-wear manufacturer, and sold her medium priced, ready-to-wear clothing in the department store Lord and Taylor. She was the first designer to use denim for dresses and made a feature of double rows of stitching and fastenings, such as hooks and eyes. Her clothing, always smart, invariably included deep side pockets, which gave a casual appearance. As footwear in the United States was strictly

Above
A shopper of 1941 presents her ration book when buying shirts. The notice on the sales counter hints at attempts to control the black market trade in coupons.

Left
One solution to the problem of the shortage of stockings.

Right
These factory-workers, seen here enjoying a lunch-break, are wearing the typical protective caps, hair nets and printed cotton overalls of the time.

Top and **left**
Two American hat designs in straw, trimmed with flowers.

Right
Accessories such as scarves became very important when new clothes were so rare. The morale boosting print by textile company Jacqmar depicts "The American Forces in London." Note also the lady on the right, who is wearing the "Stars and Stripes" tied round her hair.

rationed but ballet shoes were not, McCardell encouraged manufacturers to produce them with sturdier soles and retain the soft uppers. These became very popular with American women, who wore them with dresses and trousers. From this period onwards the fashion press, from *Vogue* down to the cheaper magazines such as *Seventeen* and *Mademoiselle*, included American designers in their fashion pages.

On February 12, 1947, Christian Dior shocked the world with his collection, which almost instantly became dubbed the "New Look." Dior's designs were a great contrast to wartime styles and created much controversy. His dresses had narrow shoulders, exaggerated busts, tiny waists, padded hips and very full skirts which reached just 12 inches from the ground. In Great Britain, there was an outcry about the extravagance of these dresses, which required up to 25 yards of material and would represent many years' worth of accumulated coupons. *Picture Post* angrily exclaimed that the "New Look" was "... launched upon a world which had not the material to copy them — and whose women have neither the money to buy, the leisure to enjoy, nor in some designs even the strength to support these masses of material."[1]

Paris had clearly re-established her position as world leader of fashion. Indeed Britain responded as if she were obliged to copy the New Look. By launching styles which Europeans could clearly not afford, Paris must have had her eye on recapturing the American market, where fabric restrictions had been lifted in 1946.

Initially, both Great Britain and the United States mocked the "New Look" and stressed its impracticalities for the housewife and typist in an age when fashion was no longer the prerogative of the rich. Against all the odds, however, women soon yearned to throw away their wartime clothes and associated memories, and adopt this new outline for the postwar era. This was harder to achieve in Europe than in the United States as rationing was not lifted until 1949 and many utility clothes remained in the shops until 1951. During this intermediary period English women did pay lip service to the "New Look" by adding a band of material to the bottom of their utility skirts to lengthen them. Even so, by 1948 wholesale versions of Christian Dior's fashion were available in many shops for those women prepared to spend many of their treasured coupons.

[1] (*Picture Post* 27.9.47, p26.)

Turned out nice again

Find time to be gay—even this busy Spring—in 'Viyella.' It'll keep you on good terms with your purse, for in spite of its soft texture and lighthearted colours 'Viyella' wears tirelessly and washes like a kitten's ear. Digby Morton—famous fashion designer—shows one way to be clever with 'Viyella'—and there are plenty more.

Viyella
REGD.
FROCK DESIGNS

Fancy Woven Designs, Checks, Stripes, Plain Shades and Marls from 6/8 yard, including Tax.

WILLIAM HOLLINS & COMPANY LIMITED · VIYELLA HOUSE · NOTTINGHAM

Left *Viyella dress, 1941.* **Bottom** *This photograph displays a new woollen stocking compared to a silk one. Manufacturers and designers combined forces to create alternatives to silk; the production of silk for clothing was banned during WWII.*

Top *A display of Utility cotton and rayon dresses. The basic design of all these garments is very similar, although some differentiation was achieved by the use of a variety of patterned fabrics.*

Top A customer makes her selection from the collection of Utility suits available, 1942.
Bottom A variety of Utility spring fashions worn by mannequins in Selfridges, 1945.

Top right The first "demobbed" men" from the RAF received civilian clothing, May 1945. Note the generous cut of these pinstriped suits, the wider lapels and cuffs on the trousers.

Far right Civilian suit designed by Major Morris May, President of the Leeds Wholesale Clothiers Federation, 1941. This had eight pockets and used only three yards of cloth, which represented a saving of 16in (40.5cm) on the average suit. This alternative was not very widely worn, however.

AMERICAN WARTIME AND POSTWAR DRESS

Left *Denim dress by Claire McCardell, 1942. This was initially intended for house and garden wear, but became so popular that its design was used for both day and evening dresses. All these photographs were taken by Louise Dahl-Wolfe for the American Harper's Bazaar, and all the clothes are by McCardell.*

Top left Full circle skirt and knitted circlet shoulder wrap, 1947. Both McCardell and Dior recognized that after the war women would welcome a complete change of style. McCardell's garments, however, were much simpler than Dior's corseted, stiff fashions. **Bottom left** Wool jersey sleeveless top and long shorts for cycling, 1949. **Above** Comfortable and classic, cotton calico summer dress, 1945. **Right** Timeless gray jersey, halter swimming costume, 1945.

EVENING DRESS

Left Evening gown by Paquin, 1946, with panier draperies on a slim sheath skirt which develops into a voluminous train.

Below Joan Crawford wearing a two piece crepe dinner dress, which she wore in the academy award-winning film Humoresque, (1946).

Right Evening gown of black Chantilly lace by Peggy Hunt of California, c. 1947.

Far right Evening dress made in a stiff but lustrous American Eastman acetate rayon, 1947.

THE "NEW LOOK"

Left A London dress manufacturer produced this dress, called "Midway," as a compromise between the old, short skirts and the new full lengths which were causing so much controversy. This dress retailed at 79s.11d — the equivalent in rationing terms of seven clothing coupons.

Right "New Look" suit, c.1947.

Above *The Duke and Duchess of Windsor, 1947. The fashion conscious Duchess is wearing the nipped-in waist and full skirted "New Look."* **Right** *At the same time that Christian Dior launched the "New Look," Jacques Fath introduced a long, lean, hobble skirted design, which was also fashionable. This garment was created by an American designer, Paul Parnes, in 1947.* **Far right** *The "New Look" at its most extreme, Christian Dior, 1947.*

Above Magazine advert, 1948, for swimwear in synthetic fibers.

Right Printed separates for American beachwear.

Left Ruched swimsuits and extra-large straw hats, 1947.

Below Mother and daughter in matching two pieces at an American beauty parade. Note the little girl's Shirley Temple curls.

Left A simple turban style hat decorated with a sword-shaped pin. **Right** Black felt turban with Bird of Paradise feathers, 1946.

Left A simple pillbox shape is adorned with spotted net, fake flowers and butterfly in this American design. **Right** An ensemble by Digby Morton for 1948. This version of the "New Look" suit is in rayon, and the extreme femininity of the style is set off with a "Dolly Varden" bonnet, giving a nostalgic feel. **Below left** Spectators at the first horseracing meeting in Paris after Liberation, in 1944, show the eccentricity that French fashion indulged in during the Occupation. **Below right** In contrast, a smart and simple American design in gray felt for 1947.

Typical fifties patterned fabrics.

CHAPTER SIX

1950
TO
1959

During the 1950s and 60s many areas of art and design — including fashion — rejected wartime values of quality and permanence. Pop Art emerged during the early 1950s and Richard Hamilton, a leading exponent, summarized this movement in 1957 when he stated that, "Pop Art is Popular, Transient, Expendable, Low Cost, Mass Produced, Young, Witty, Sexy, Gimmicky, Glamorous, Big Business."[1]

Pop artists wholeheartedly embraced commercial — and particularly American — culture, and promoted the idea that comic and packaging art was as valid as traditional fine art forms. Rock 'n 'Roll, which started in the United States, hit the world by the mid-1950s and was enthusiastically consumed by the relatively affluent and increasingly visible teenage market. Audrey Hepburn, Marilyn Monroe and, by the late 1950s, Brigitte Bardot were the most popular and widely copied film stars of the period. Lana Turner also influenced dress. She became known as the "Sweater Girl" for the tight fitting jumpers she wore over bras which were reinforced with stiffening points, and helped to create the vogue for knitwear. James Dean's and Marlon Brando's denim and leather clothing became almost universally adopted by young men. The United States economy had been thriving since the war, and by the mid 1950s the United Kingdom, too, was enjoying a period of full employment. Between 1945 and 1958 world manufacturers of consumer goods increased by 60 per cent. The dual income family became increasingly common and this rise in income, coupled with the rapid extension in credit and rent-to-buy facilities, greatly expanded the market for consumer goods and clothing.

Technology became a dominant force throughout the 1950s and 60s and was seen to symbolize the modern world. Technological developments were welcomed with excitement as they optimistically promised to transform lives, and consumer durables in particular promised to liberate the busy woman from housework. Many major strides were also made in the production of synthetic fibers, which became a great asset to the 1950s wardrobe. Nylon, which arrived from the United States after the war, was invaluable for the manufacture of tights and underwear. Other trademarked fabrics included Aurilan, Banlon and Orlon, all of which were easily washed, dripped dry and did not require ironing. As a result, thick synthetic sweaters and suits manufactured in light colors became very popular, although a later return to natural fibers made them redundant by the 1970s.

In Paris, Dior designed a variety of intricately cut and highly sophisticated couture garments. In 1951 he created the Princess line, in 1954 the long-waisted H line, and the A and Y lines in 1957, when he also designed the first chemise dresses. These began the long fashion for loose fitting clothing which Yves Saint Laurent, Dior's assistant, designed after his death in the same year. Chanel, who had

closed her doors in 1939, reopened her salon in 1954, and continued to design classical, comfortable clothing for her customers, in contrast to Dior's garments, which quickly dated. During this period, she designed the famous Chanel suit — just-below-the-knee length skirt, and round-necked

Above left
Marilyn Monroe, the ultimate sex symbol, was as well loved by women as she was by men. Both during her lifetime and after her death, hundreds of women have copied her style. She's pictured here in 1954.

Above right
Jayne Mansfield was a "dumb blonde" in the Monroe mould, who successfully parodied Hollywood's depiction of women whilst being a part of the system. This photo is from 1957.

Left
Richard Hamilton compiled this collage, entitled Just What Is It That Makes Today's Homes So Different, So Appealing? from American advertisements in 1956.

Right
London Teddy Boy, 1954.

jacket trimmed in a contrasting color braid. As in the 1920s, her clothing was widely copied by all grades of manufacturer. Balenciaga, Fath, Rochas and Balmain were also among the leading couturiers of the period, all of whom depended on the talents of Irving Penn, John French and Richard Avedon, top fashion photographers who captured the elegance of their clothes for *Vogue* and *Harpers*. In Great Britain, the fashions of Norman Hartnell, Hardy Amies and Victor Stiebel were internationally admired, as were the exquisite sculptural evening gowns of New York designer Charles James.

During the 1950s the couture trade began to decline as top quality, ready-to-wear clothing became increasingly available. For financial reasons, many couturiers designed for chain stores and manufacturers: Amies designed prototypes for Hepworths and Debenhams; Hartnell designed for Berkertex. The couture industry has always dressed large numbers of influential women free of charge, and therefore spin-offs such as the sale of perfumes and accessories have boosted their profits and often kept them in business.

The style of men's clothing changed dramatically during the 1950s. After an initially formal start, men's dress relaxed considerably as the conventional shirt and tie was sometimes replaced with a sweater, and separates became widely worn. Savile Row and Jermyn Street in London had always led the world in menswear, but in 1957, when John Stephen opened his first shop in Carnaby Street, this too became internationally established for its cheaper high fashion clothing.

In 1950, British *Vogue* reported that, "There is a new almost Edwardian formality in men's London clothes, which is reminiscent of the pre-1914 period."[2] This had been a glorious period for the English upper class and one which many undoubtedly wished to revive. The "New Edwardians," as they became known, adopted stove-pipe trousers, high, stiff white collars, and patterned vests, but by 1954 the term "Teddy Boy" was interchangeable with "New Edwardian": a group of working class youths had adopted cheaper and more elaborate versions of the style. *Punch* stated that, "Crimes are now committed, on fashionable commons, by young gentlemen in the velvet collars and fancy waistcoats, the turned-up cuffs and buttoned-down pockets of the Edwardian masher."[3]

According to many people, "Teds" were involved in racist attacks and petty larceny, and their clothes became synonymous with their crimes: they wore their collars turned up or tied down with boot-lace ties, tight draped trousers and heavy crepe-soled "brothel creepers" on their feet; their hair was long, and they used grease to style variously shaped quiffs. Although Teddy Boys consisted of only a minority of individuals, they reflected the increasing confidence and financial independence that enabled young people to express themselves through their dress

101

during the 1950s. For the first time, teenagers donned different clothing from that worn by their parents and fashion became a youthful phenomenon.

In great contrast to the stylized artificiality of the Teds, most young men and women adopted more casual clothing. Many teenage girls wore drainpipe trousers, big sweaters and flat pumps and for evening a full circle skirt with a turtle neck sweater. It was jeans, however, which transformed the appearance of the 1950s teenager. Denim was first used for trousers by Levi Strauss, when it provided hard wearing and cheap work clothing for American gold miners during the mid-nineteenth century. From then onwards it was used to make men's and boy's bib overalls for work, and was used by the American armed forces throughout World War II. However, the huge demand for jeans and dungarees which emerged from men, women and children, but mainly from teenagers, during the 1950s was sparked off by films when James Dean wore jeans in *Rebel without a Cause* (1955), and Elvis Presley wore a denim suit in *Jailhouse Rock* (1957). Although jeans have often been credited as being truly democratic clothing, they have, like other fashion garments, always had to be of

Above
Working class teenagers at a dancehall.

Left
Teddy Boy in Bristol, 1955.

Right
Audrey Hepburn epitomized a chic, gamine style. She was frequently dressed by Givenchy, who also designed the costumes for her best known film, Funny Face.

Far right
This stand at the Ideal Home Exhibition of 1956 represented the designers' predictions for furnishings and fashions of 1980.

the "right" brand and style.

In 1955 Bazaar was opened on the King's Road, London, by Mary Quant and her husband Alexander Plunket Green and heralded the dominance of the British boutique. Quant went on to become one of the many art school-trained designers who radically changed the face of fashion and established London as a major fashion center. As she could not find the fashions she wanted to retail, Quant designed and, initially, made her stock. She and her husband already mixed socially with the much spotlighted "Chelsea Set," who formed a large part of their initial clientele and helped to publicize her garments: within one week of opening, Bazaar took more than five times the amount of money anticipated. Mary Quant and Alexander Plunket Green proved both to themselves and the clothing trades at large that there existed a huge demand for fashionable clothing from the young which reached its peak during the 1960s.

[1](Hamilton, Richard, *Collected Works 1953-77,* Thames & Hudson, London, 1982, p28.)
[2](*Vogue,* April 1950, p109.)
[3](*Punch,* February 24, 1954, p268.)

SUITS AND COATS

Left *Suit, Nina Ricci, 1951. Black and white houndstooth suit with astrakan cuffs, developing into a muff.* **Top left** *Suit, Jacques Fath, 1951. Black wool suit trimmed with mink.* **Top** *Wool suits, 1957, showing the popular "stand away" neckline.*

Top *Duster style coat, designed by Adele of California c.1955.* **Right** *Coat by Pierre Balmain, 1951. This full skirted coat had a hemline with a circumference of 12ft. The waistline silhouette is formed by a series of darts that throw pleats above and below the waistline.*

Left *A two-piece gray silk suit from the House of Christian Dior, 1957.*

105

DRESSES

Right *American debutantes on being presented to the Queen in 1955. The last presentation of debs was in 1958.* **Below** *Afternoon dresses by Yves Saint Laurent for Christian Dior, 1958. The two dresses on the left are in printed silk, the one on the right in fine black wool.*

Left *Printed cotton summer dress, 1956.*

Left A dress in coral pink wool by the House of Worth, 1956. **Right** A spotted sundress.

Left *Green, swathed evening dress by Christian Dior, 1959.*

Left *Off-white doeskin wool by the House of Worth, 1955. This earliest of fashion houses was controlled by members of the Worth family until 1954, when they were bought out by the House of Paquin.*

Left Ballgown in white tulle, scattered with yellow flowers and with large green bustle-bow, Norman Hartnell, 1954. Hartnell is best known for his designs for the Queen (particularly her wedding dress, and coronation robe) and Winterhalter-inspired crinolines, like the one seen here, were his forte. **Bottom left** Evening dress and coat by Jacques Fath, 1956. Fath started his career in 1937, and was a key name in the immediate postwar period. After his death in 1954, his wife Genevieve kept the House open until 1957 **Right** Evening coat by top British ready-to-wear company, Berkertex, 1957, in a synthetic satin fabric.

THE TEEN MARKET

See you later Alligator

The teen market became very important in the affluent environment of the late 1950s. **Far left** A 1957 collection showing the "acceptable" face of Rock'n'Roll styles, achieved with a liberal use of synthetic fibers such as nylon net and taffeta. **Left** This shows a more disreputable and down-market version — notice particularly the stiletto heeled shoes. There were attempts made to ban these from public venues because of the damage they did to floor surfaces.

Center The Beatniks of the late 50s mixed influences from the Left Bank Paris set and American jazz performers. Their dress reflected a deliberate rejection of consumer values, and the free and easy lifestyle documented by Allen Ginsburg and Jack Kerouac. Ironically, many of the styles they favored have become fashion classics, such as the check shirt, "sloppy-joe" sweater, and black dirndl skirt. **Top left** Teddy Tinling separates of 1957. The girl's T-shirt cashes in on the popularity of British pop singer Tommy Steele. **Left** These jive fans wear practical clothes for dancing.

111

CASUAL WEAR

Peggy Page COTTON SUNDRESS
and button-to-waist jacket, in bright Mexican inspired print. The dress has detachable shoulder straps and its own underskirt.
Colours: **PINK/BLUE, RED/OLIVE.**
Sizes: 36", 38", 40", 42" hips.

B.624 **84/-** or 12/6 monthly

SAIL CLOTH DRESS
buttoned through, with white saddle stitching to match pearl effect buttons. Huge patch pockets.
Colours: **DEEP ROSE PINK, ATLANTIC BLUE.**
Sizes: 36", 38", 40" hips.

B.623 **£4.19.6** or 15/- monthly

Linzi SUNDRESS AND FITTED JACKET
Flower print cotton dress. Empire line bodice, full skirt. Midi jacket has detachable belt.
Colours: **WHITE/BLUE, WHITE/PINK.**
Sizes: 34", 36", 38", 40" hips.

B.625 **£6.16.6** or 21/- monthly

Page 9

Top left *Skirts and sweaters, Autumn, 1954.* **Bottom left** *Teenage spectators at Wimbledon 1953 show aspirations of Hollywood glamor with their sunglasses, strapless bodices, waspie belts and bangles.*

Above *1957 mail order: printed cotton sundresses.*

Right *These separates combine a strange mix of space-age and ethnic themes by Teddy Tinling, 1958.* **Far right** *Italian separates in mohair, 1958.*

MEN AND CHILDREN

Top left *1951 styles for teenagers in new synthetic fibers. The boy is wearing a terylene/wool blend suit, terylene shirt, socks and tie; and she is in all nylon: dress, socks, ballet pumps and fake fur wrap.*
Bottom left *A large family of 1955, the girls in typical cotton dresses.*
Above *An ensemble by Kay Lewis of California... but...* **Right** *in reality, the crumpled cotton dress and battered sun hat was more common. This photo is from 1959.*

Right *Designers attempted to ring the changes on the traditional theme with printed jacket linings, or cut away jackets, 1957.*

Above *Menswear of 1959: single breasted three piece suits in check fabrics.* **Right** *Marlon Brando presented an alternative image for young men. Here, he is wearing the leather jacket and blue jeans he popularized in the film,* The Wild One *(1953).*

SWIMWEAR AND UNDERWEAR

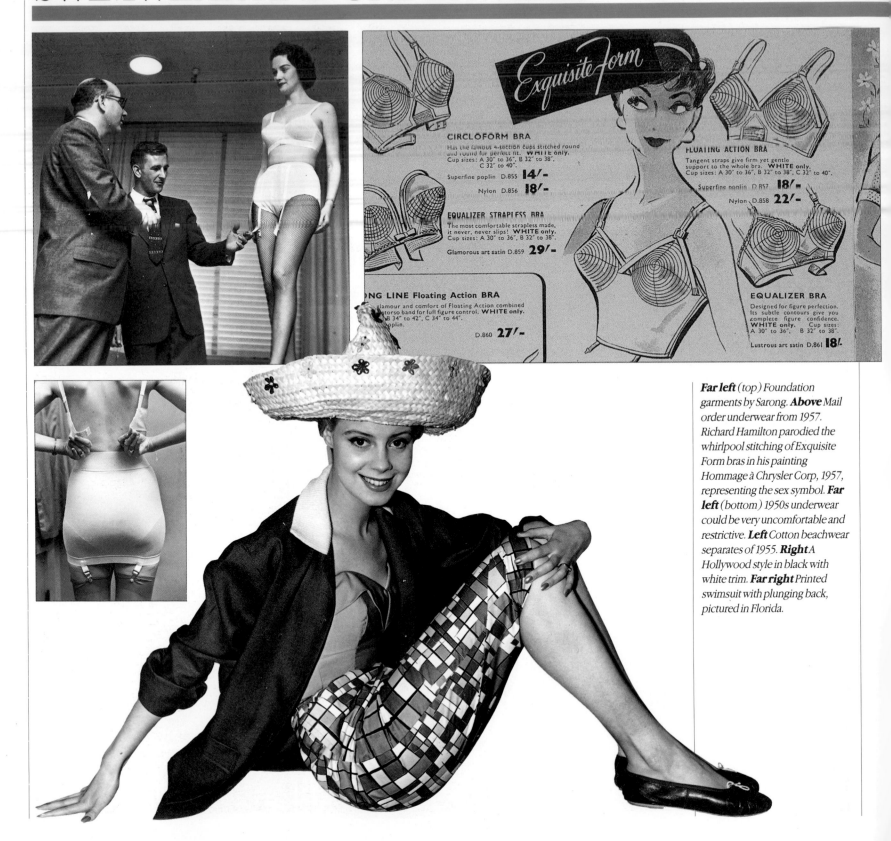

Exquisite Form

CIRCLOFORM BRA
Has the famous 4-section cups stitched round and round for perfect fit. **WHITE** only.
Cup sizes: A 30" to 36", B 32" to 38", C 32" to 40".
Superfine poplin D.855 **14/-**
Nylon D.856 **18/-**

FLOATING ACTION BRA
Tangent straps give firm yet gentle support to the whole bra. **WHITE** only.
Cup sizes: A 30" to 36", B 32" to 38", C 32" to 40".
Superfine poplin D.857 **18/-**
Nylon D.858 **22/-**

EQUALIZER STRAPLESS BRA
The most comfortable strapless made, it never, never slips! **WHITE** only.
Cup sizes: A 30" to 36", B 32" to 38".
Glamorous art satin D.859 **29/-**

NG LINE Floating Action BRA
glamour and comfort of Floating Action combined torso band for full figure control. **WHITE** only.
B 34" to 42", C 34" to 44".
poplin.
D.860 **27/-**

EQUALIZER BRA
Designed for figure perfection. Its subtle contours give you complete figure confidence. **WHITE** only. Cup sizes: A 30" to 36", B 32" to 38".
Lustrous art satin D.861 **18/-**

Far left (top) Foundation garments by Sarong. **Above** Mail order underwear from 1957. Richard Hamilton parodied the whirlpool stitching of Exquisite Form bras in his painting Hommage à Chrysler Corp, 1957, representing the sex symbol. **Far left** (bottom) 1950s underwear could be very uncomfortable and restrictive. **Left** Cotton beachwear separates of 1955. **Right** A Hollywood style in black with white trim. **Far right** Printed swimsuit with plunging back, pictured in Florida.

HATS

Above Although fashion in the 1950s was becoming more informal, a social occasion still demanded a hat. This 1957 design is one of the more elegant and upmarket hats on offer.

Right Traditional milliners in the 1950s could still hold their own against the mass manufactured hat, a situation that was soon to change. This showroom display of 1955 demonstrates a preponderance of small, mostly brimless, hats.

Above A 1955 design by society milliner Gina Davies is very characteristic of the period — small, smart and understated.

This black velvet hat with grosgrain trim shows one of the elegant and aristocratic styles popular in the 1950s. British models such as Barbara Goalen characterized this look.

"Is Paris dead?" design by Pierre Cardin.

CHAPTER·SEVEN

1960
TO
1969

During the 1960s the media played a major role in creating mass markets for goods and used fashion as a marketing device to redefine constantly consumer tastes. This built-in obsolescence reached its peak with the brief vogue for fashionably styled throwaway paper dresses and inflatable plastic furniture. Television and car ownership, which had increased during the 1950s, accelerated rapidly, greatly reducing variations within and between countries, and increasing personal mobility. Much has been made of the introduction of the contraceptive pill and the "permissive society," but a great deal of deep-rooted Victorian moralism also existed. This was highlighted by the much-publicized court case in 1963 concerning the explicitly sexual passages in D.H. Lawrence's novel, *Lady Chatterley's Lover*.

The dominant fashion retail outlet of the 1960s was the boutique, which provided a conducive selling environment for the young — gimmicky interiors, loud pop music and a self-service approach — but this decade also witnessed a rapid expansion in chain store trading for cheap and medium priced garments. Textile design was greatly influenced by Op Art between 1960 and 1967. Op — short for optical — Art played on visual responses to abstract paintings which appeared to ripple, project or recede, although the painting was static and the surface two-dimensional. These were often monochrome, but also juxtaposed colored hues to achieve a similar effect. Bridget Riley, Richard Anuszkiewicz, Peter Sedgley and Piero Dorazio were the leading artists of this important, although marginal, art movement.

Fashion during the 1960s was mainly British led, but the styles had repercussions around the world. In 1961 Mary Quant opened her second boutique in Knightsbridge, and a year later was designing garments for J C Penney's 1,700 American chain stores. Quant, Plunkett-Green and their financial advisor Archie McNair combined a great talent for design with outstanding business acumen. By 1964 Quant was designing paper patterns for Butterick, which made the styles of her medium priced garments available to a wider market, 1966 saw the start of Quant's cosmetic empire, and by the 1970s her daisy logo promoted a huge range of items including stationery, bed linen and toys. Quant designed mini-skirts, hipster flared trousers, gym suits and fun furs for the young. As hemlines rose — sometimes to thigh level — brightly colored and textured tights became very fashionable, and were another area in which Quant designed under license.

Barbara Hulanicki and her husband Stephen Fitz-Simon, who was her business manager, also made a significant contribution to 60s fashion. She started her career selling cheap, mail-order fashion clothes which she advertised in the press to the teenage market. The demand for these was phenomenal, and in 1963 she opened her first boutique, called Biba. In contrast to the many bright colors of the 60s,

Biba clothes were made in muted mauves, prunes, blues, greys, pinks and black. Her high-fashion clothing cost a fraction of Quant's and was consumed within minutes of going on display. Far from looking sexually provocative in their skimpy clothing, Quant's and Hulanicki's customers often assumed a child-like appearance and by the late 60s Twiggy and Maddy Smith's

Above

Men's clothes in the 1960s demonstrated a freedom in the use of colours and fabrics never seen before or since in this century. The shirt here is of embroidered cotton voile from the London Boutique, Mr Fish.

Top left

Coat by Biba, in characteristic dusky colours.

Bottom left

The music and appearance of the pop group, The Beatles dominated the decade. In the early 1960s, their haircuts were considered to be daringly long and their Italian-inspired suits spawned numerous high-street copies.

Top right

Mary Quant launching a range of her shoe designs in the early 1960s.

Bottom right

Brightly coloured evening dress with label, "Light Years Ahead".

123

Above

The Mod style — Italian suits, parkas, short, sharp haircuts and the all-important Italian (Vespa) scooter — seen here at a rally. The violence that often accompanied such meetings kept the image of the Mods in the newspapers.

teenage figures became the fashionable ideal: a strong contrast to the shapely and more mature physique fashionable during the 1950s.

The Chelsea spirit was witnessed in Paris too — not in the quiet salons of Dior or Balenciaga, but from the new houses of André Courrèges and Paco Rabanne. The widespread interest in space throughout the decade was reflected in the garments of these designers. Paco Rabanne and Courrèges used unconventional materials, such as plastics and metals, and silver and white were predominant. Andy Warhol, the American pop artist, loved Courrèges' clothes and proposed that everyone should look the same, dressed in silver, as that merged into a futuristic technological environment. The dictatorship of Parisian couture upon mass-clothing styles began to crumble as the new generation of young London designers largely dominated the field. Nina Ricci, Lanvin and Yves Saint Laurent opened ready-to-wear boutiques to broaden their market.

Men's clothing broke down barriers about what was

considered acceptable or effeminate, as designers challenged men to wear pink, flower-patterned shirts. Mick Jagger, lead singer of pop group The Rolling Stones, defied convention when he went on stage wearing a white organdie mini-dress over trousers. Teddy boys had largely died out (although small groups retained the style and are still evident today), and by 1963, Mods and Rockers became the dominant sub-cultural groups in Britain. Mods were acutely fashion conscious and adopted Parka coats, smart and fairly tight-fitting Italian suits, shirts with button-down collars and winklepicker or hushpuppy shoes. For casual clothes, Levi jeans, Fred Perry sports shirts and cardigans were worn, and Mod girls dressed in knitted twin-sets, shift dresses, ski-pants and suits with straight skirts which reached three inches below the knee. Much of the Mods' clothing was bought from boutiques in Carnaby Street. The Vespa motor scooter became central to their group identity and these, adorned with flags and mascots, provided the transport to seaside resorts where they fought bitter battles with their opponents, the Rockers. The latter, in complete contrast, were disinterested in fashion and wore old jeans and leathers and rode high-powered motor-bikes.

Hippies formed a radically different group in the 1960s. Self-contained, they rejected the commercialism of the 60s culture and were in sympathy with the rising peace movement. Their ethnic styles of clothing, such as Afghan coats, kaftans, Indian fringed belts, headbands and beads, were bought from the newly opened Indian boutiques; they wore their hair long, and often painted their bodies with flowers and psychedelic patterns. From 1967 until the early 70s, peasant styles became very fashionable among more conventional circles.

By 1969 the highly successful American designer Rudi Geinrich stated that, "Haute couture doesn't have the same meaning any more because money, status and power no longer have the same meaning. Now fashion starts in the streets. What I do is watch what kids are putting together for themselves. I formalize it, give it something of my own, perhaps, and then it is fashion."[1]

This filtering up, as opposed to down, of designs became a significant factor in 1970s dress.

[1] (*Fortune*, January 1969, p87.)

Above

Designs in black leather and printed silk by Pierre Cardin, 1969. Cardin presented his first collection in his own name in 1953 and became known for "unisex" designs. He has since become famous, if not notorious, for attaching his name to almost every conceivable consumer product — from towels to luggage and even furniture.

Top left

As those involved in the hippy subculture became increasingly interested in Eastern cultures and religions, and traveled to India to sit at the feet of gurus, they adopted textiles and jewelry from the Third World.

Left

The unorthodox materials that Paco Rabanne favored for his clothes led to bizarre methods of manufacture. Here he is seen wielding a pair of pliers to construct a chain-mail dress — a process more akin to sculpture than dressmaking.

125

SUITS

Left Woven Courtelle wool tweed suit by Alexon, 1962. Alexon, a British company still in existence, sells quality medium priced garments to a largely middle class market. Their clothes are sold in department stores. **Bottom left** Mrs Kennedy, wife of the then President of the United States, 1961. Jackie Kennedy was a highly visible and widely copied fashion consumer during the 1960s.

Below Stretch-towelling catsuits, 1967. These hooded suits demonstrate an easily wearable example of the influence of space exploration on fashion.

Right Publicity shot for the London showing of Yves St. Laurent's Spring Collection, 1963.

Left Tweed suit by Marc Bohan, chief designer at Christian Dior, 1966. Photograph by Cecil Beaton. **Right** White lace mini-skirted suit, photographed at Ascot, 1966. By this date the mini had become widely accepted, even in the conventional setting of Ascot. This woman's escort is dressed, in great contrast, in Edwardian attire. **Below** Twiggy and Justin de Villeneuve at the Ritz Hotel, London, c. 1969.

DRESSES

Above Smart, geometric mid-1960s styles. **Top right** These designs are by John Bates for a popular television series, The Avengers, in 1965. .

Right In 1963 Mary Quant launched her Ginger Group range of cheap, interchangeable pieces. This selection from 1965 shows mix-and-match red sweaters with camel and red pinafore dresses or skirts. **Far right** A 1966 white tabard dress with printed sleeves and tights (in Bri-Nylon).

Top left As designers became bored with the ubiquitous mini, they began to experiment with new lengths. These two "maxi" dresses are by Pierre Cardin, 1969.

Left (bottom) Cotton lace by top British ready-to-wear company Frank Usher, 1968.

Above Barbara Hulanicki started designing and manufacturing under the name Biba in 1964. This is a later style made in printed Tricel.

COATS

Bottom right In this 1962 design, Paco Rabanne demonstrates his experimental approach to materials and manufacturing. Made from small pieces of cut leather, it is joined together by studs to give a chain mail effect.

Above In 1965 the Sunday Telegraph magazine asked, "Is Paris Dead?," reflecting the lessening influence of haute couture. But these smart and simple coats by Marc Bohan for Dior are classic, stylish design. **Left** This sunshine yellow design with contrasting black collar and button trim characterizes the bold use of color that exemplified the best of 60s fashion.

Top right *A smart geometric design of 1965.* **Far right** *A glamorous (if impractical) suit by Biba, 1968, of white moire coat and trousers.* **Bottom left** *The informality of the 60s allowed the winter coat to be abandoned for a more casual style, such as a long, knitted cardigan: this example, from 1969, is in Shetland wool.*

131

CASUAL WEAR

Left Bowling outfits in stretch nylon by Teddy Tinling, 1962. **Bottom left** Knitted separates in Bri-Nylon yarns, 1963. **Below** Printed separates.

Right Audience at a late 1960s Pop Festival. **Far right** (top) The influence of the military theme as seen in London's Portobello Road. **Far right** (bottom) The blouse on the left, and both pairs of slacks, are made of synthetic Dacron/rayon fabrics. The tunic on the right is in screen-printed linen from 1966.

EVENING DRESS

Left Classical ballgown by the House of Givenchy, which opened in 1952. **Center** Op Art designs in silk jersey, 1966. **Bottom** Balmain evening dresses, 1966. The House of Balmain opened in 1946 and was immensely popular throughout the 1950s and 60s.

Right The rainwear company Burberry launched its knitwear collection in 1966 with these see through, handknitted designs in gold mesh. **Far right** A characteristically inventive design by Paco Rabanne, 1967, in silvered leather.

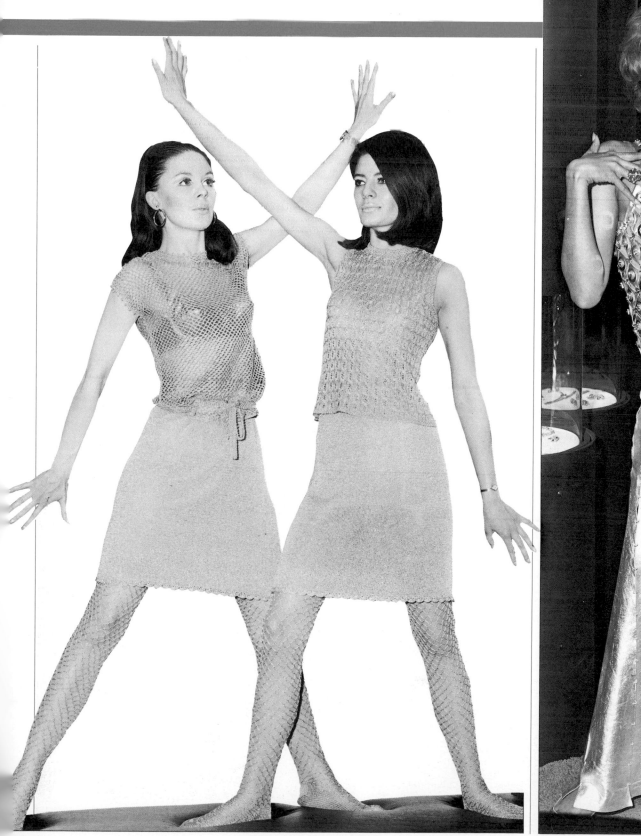

135

SWIMWEAR AND UNDERWEAR

Right Underwear by Kayser Bondor for 1966. A bolder use of color and pattern was made by this date than in the 1950s. These styles are for a slightly older woman, as by the mid 60s most young women would have preferred tights to stockings and suspenders. **Below** Nylon underwear, 1967, in "fun" styles made of synthetic fabrics.

Far left These pantie girdles may have "pop" motifs printed on them, but they demonstrate that even in the easy going 1960s some women felt the need of "supportive" underwear to assist a fashionably stick like look. **Left** A design for topless bathing by Rudi Geinrich. **Below** Swimwear suggesting the influence of the James Bond film, Dr No.

CHILDREN

Left *A variety of styles from 1965.* **Far left** *(bottom) These boys' and girls' suits of 1968 were launched to introduce a new crease resistant fabric by the Courtaulds company.* **Bottom left** *Pierre Cardin repeated the space-age look for children's clothes in 1967.*

Right *These boys from the late 60s wear the fringed vests and flares that were fashionable for men.* **Far right** *(top) Boys' and girls' party wear in black velvet from the Baby Dior range, 1968.* **Far right** *(bottom) Printed velvet maxi-length coats, 1969.*

MEN

Top left Blazer by John Stephen, c.1965, worn with white shirt and flowery tie. Stephen, whose main shop was in Carnaby Street, became one of the leading fashion designers for men in the 1960s. **Above** This photograph shows everyday, casual menswear, 1967. **Left** The Beatles wearing hippy style clothing, c. 1967.

Opposite page. Left Union Jack jacket, c. 1965. **Top right** Fashions from Cecil Gee, one of Britain's high street retailers. 1966. **Bottom right** Italian menswear, designed by the house of Ellesse, Perugia, 1969.

141

HAIR AND HATS

Left and **far left** Two designs from mass manufacturer Edward Mann, 1966. **Bottom left** Hats for men and women, 1961.

Left Fun spectacle designs, 1964, in plastic and diamanté. **Bottom left** Caps of imitation flowers, 1963. **Bottom right** Victoriana styles by fashionable hairdresser Raymond "Mr Teasy-Weasy," 1969. False hairpieces were popular throughout the 60s.

Sequinned glamor by Bruce Oldfield, 1979.

CHAPTER EIGHT

1970
TO
1979

The optimistic spirit of the 1960s began to fade in the 1970s with high inflation, rising unemployment and growing dissatisfaction with industrial life and technology. In his influential book *Design For the Real World* (1972), Victor Papanek stressed that the designer had a responsibility to provide for real human needs — particularly those of the disabled, and of underdeveloped countries — rather than to conceive trashy, ephemeral goods. Likewise, the Craft Revival in design, which emphasized the beauty of handmade and individual items, rejected mass produced popular culture. The great vogue for peasant styles of dress during the late 1960s and early 1970s was perhaps indicative of the growing interest in health foods, ecology and world peace. The carefully marketed goods from Body Shop International, whose beauty products have been made from natural substances and tested without cruelty to animals since the 1970s, commercially reiterate this mood. The women's movement also gained considerable momentum during this decade, fueled by the publication of Germaine Greer's feminist book *The Female Eunuch* (1970).

1970 was a year of contradictory dress styles. Some women wore their hair in the mode of the Pre-Raphaelites and assumed long, ethereal dresses, while others shortened their mini-skirts even further. During the early years of the decade fashion did not change radically from that worn in the 60s. Shorts with bibs or straps, which became dubbed "hotpants," provided some variation to the ubiquitous mini-skirts, which were available in a variety of materials: cotton, satin, leather, suede, velvet, corduroy and sometimes knitted or crocheted. At the same time, and in great contrast, Laura Ashley designed her very popular cotton Edwardian-style dresses with high collars and puffed sleeves; many of her fabrics were printed from simple, floral motifs based upon eighteenth and nineteenth century designs.

The 1973 opening of the Biba emporium in Kensington High Street was to become the last symbol of London's swinging Sixties. A staggering £5 million were spent on re-building and decorating this store to Barbara Hulanicki's personal style, and the result was an eclectic combination of Victorian Art Nouveau and Art Deco mixed with Hollywood glamour. The woodwork was painted dark-brown, mirrors were peach-tinted, and peacock-backed basket chairs provided seating for the customers. Leopardskin rugs, feather boas and lilies created the store's decadent ambience, and Biba's reputation was such that it was the first boutique to risk mysterious blacked out windows which did not promote the store's merchandise. Biba sold men's, women's and children's fashions, food, and objects for interiors.

Hulanicki sold a packaged lifestyle where wit and style took precedence over sales drives: her merchandise covered only 90,000 out of a possible 200,000 square feet.

Above
Hotpants were the favourite fashion for the young in 1971, but an impossible style for anyone out of their teens or not so slim.

Left
Interest in the cultures of developing countries continued to be a dominant theme throughout much of the 1970s.

Right and **Below**
The Biba premises in London, remarkable for — among other things — its dark, dramatic decor.

Shortly after the opening, Alistair Best was moved to remark in *Design* magazine that "...shopping is almost a fringe activity." In the food hall, dog food was stored in the belly of a giant Great Dane shaped stand and yet there were only a couple of checkouts. It irked British Land, Biba's backers, to see that people were soaking up the environment without feeling any obligation to buy. Hulanicki was an enormously talented designer but she suffered from stock-control and security problems as well as from an urge to fulfill her own retailing ideals, even at the expense of lost profits. British Land tried to commercialize and functionalize Biba, but in so doing drained the store of its life and appreciative public. Biba closed its doors in 1975 with losses of £6 million and was taken over as premises for Marks & Spencer.

Throughout the 1970s jeans continued to be widely worn, as indeed they are to the present day, although their shape, color depth and decoration has changed with fashion. During the early 1970s denims which flared from the knee down and became faded with age were the most desirable — so much so that a second-hand pair often cost

more than a new one. Embroidered and patched jeans were also very fashionable, and dungarees enjoyed popularity throughout the decade. Many of America's leading ready-to-wear designers, including Ralph Lauren, Calvin Klein and Perry Ellis, regularly included denim in their collections and produced status-loaded "designer jeans."

Punk, initially confined to a group of mainly unemployed youths, emerged in Great Britain in the summer of 1976. Their dispiritedness was heightened and excited by Malcolm McLaren who managed and hyped the Sex Pistols band. Punk aimed to shock, and defiantly contradicted accepted modes of beauty and behavior. At its most extreme, black plastic bin liners parodied garments, toilet chains became necklaces, and razor blades and safety pins were worn as multiple earrings. Existing garments were made to look more fragmented with slashes and crudely and loosely knitted mohair sweaters were widely worn. Punks' acidic-colored and carefully spiked hair and their bizarre, disheveled appearances highlighted their rebellion, poverty and leisure.

Vivienne Westwood, McLaren's partner, dressed the "well-off" punks and many art students. Their store in the Kings Road assumed many names throughout the 1970s: in 1971, "Let It Rock" used styles based upon Teddy Boy clothes; in 1972 "Too Young To Live, Too Fast To Die" sold James Dean-inspired clothing; 1974's "Sex" sold fetishistic and rubber garments; in 1977, "Seditionaries: Clothes For Heroes" sold punk clothing; and in 1980 it was changed to "World's End." In 1977 the price of a pair of bondage trousers in black cotton, with a loin cloth or kilt, from Seditionaries was £30.00, more than one weeks' social security for many punks, and consequently completely out of reach. The punk image could be easily achieved, however, by buying second hand garments and dyeing them black, dyeing and spiking the hair, and using black cosmetics. Period clothing and American surplus stores have enjoyed great patronage since the 1970s, especially from teenagers and students seeking a cheap and individual style.

As the decade progressed, the imagery of punk was commercialized, upgraded and filtered into mainstream fashion and couture. This took many forms, but the most noticeable were the widespread appearance of loosely-woven, unstructured garments, boiler suits, superfluous zippers, and back-brushed and spiky hairstyles. Decorative safety pins and razor blades sold in boutiques as cheap fashion jewelry, and in many jewelry stores fashioned in gold. Men and women also had numerous holes pierced in their ears.

Above

Managed by Malcolm McLaren and clothed by McLaren and Vivienne Westwood, punk band the Sex Pistols initiated a revolution in both the music and fashion industries.

Far right

Zandra Rhodes has produced clothes of a unique glamor since 1968. Usually her designs proclaim her highly individual signature; in 1977, however, she used the imagery and motifs common to punk street fashion to produce hybrids such as this ripped-and-pinned silk jersey dress.

Right

Many young women in Britain in the late 1970s adopted a style which showed the influence of the singer from the band, Siouxsie and the Banshees.

Fiorucci was one of the many fashion stores which sold punk-inspired clothing for the young. The first Fiorucci was opened in Milan, Italy, in the mid 1960s and came to London in 1968 where it stocked fashions by London's young designers; by the mid 1970s Fiorucci was selling many exciting garments which made much use of plastics and fluorescent colors, and others based upon 1950s styles. At the top level, Zandra Rhodes introduced and romanticized punk into the privileged world of couture.

During the 1970s Milan became a recognized new capital of fashion. Italian clothing designers, such as Simonetta, Fontana and Cappuci, had started to make a name for themselves from the mid 1950s, but with little impact internationally. Giorgio Armani, who has become one of Milan's leading ready-to-wear designers for men and women, set up his own company in 1975, having previously worked as a designer for the menswear manufacturer Nino Cerruti and as an independent fashion consultant. Armani has introduced ease and comfort into classic, tailored garments — favoring items which look a little worn or crumpled when new — and makes much use of linen.

DRESSES

Far left (*top*) Lee Bender designed young, cheap clothes for her chain of Bus Stop boutiques from 1968-1979. This purple printed crepe is from 1970. **Far left** (*bottom*) An ethnic inspired outfit by Monsoon Fashions, 1974. **Left** Rust wool overdress worn with black pants, Dior Boutique, 1978. **Below** "Gipsy" style dress by Ossie Clark for Quorum, 1970. **Right** A characteristic design by Jean Muir in fluid printed chiffon. In 1962 Muir worked under the label "Jane and Jane" before launching her own company in 1966.

Above A puff sleeved mini by Mary Quant's Ginger Group, 1972. **Below** Fabrics designed by Mary Quant in crimplene for ICI, 1975.

151

SUITS AND COATS

Right Knitted suit, maxi length coat and cap, c.1974.

Right Mary Quant's Ginger Group suit, 1972.

Left Knitted jacket and wool coat worn with thigh length boots, 1975.

Left Jeff Banks' "Punk Style" double-breasted Mitchum jacket and skirt, 1977. Jeff Banks' high fashion was, and is today, immensely popular. **Right** Top quality knickerbocker suit, with vest in wool and cashmere, 1978.

153

EVENING DRESS

Below *Mary Quant lurex and paper taffeta mini-dress with double sleeves, 1972. This, like many 70s clothes, could have been worn during the day or evening.*

Top right *A fluid Jean Patou evening outfit, 1976.* **Bottom left** *Bill Gibb evening dress, c.1977.* **Bottom right** *Ossie Clarke tunic and trousers, c.1973, photographed by Helmut Newton.*

Far left Sculptured evening dress by the Japanese designer Yuki, c.1972. **Left** Yves St. Laurent's ethnic styles, 1976. **Below** Halter-neck evening dress from Norman Hartnell's "Petit Salon," which was aimed at a younger clientele, 1972.

CASUAL WEAR

Left Hotpants suited the active, liberated, youthful image of women in the early 1970s. Photograph by David Bailey, 1971. **Above** Another example of hotpants as witnessed in the Kings Road, Chelsea, 1971.

Above *The ultra wide flared trousers that epitomize the early part of the decade.* **Left** *Indian cotton dungarees were another 1970s favorite.*

Left *Vivienne Westwood with bleached, cropped hair and simple baggy T-shirt, 1977. This look was widely adopted by the young.*
Right *The influence of Ralph Lauren's designs for Woody Allen's film Annie Hall (1978) can be seen in this layered jacket and crumpled socks.*

PUNK

Opposite page. Far left
Skinhead boy and punk girl wearing spider knit jumper, leather mini, ripped fishnet stockings and heavy boots. **Top center** *Punk girl with her cheek pierced, and chains hanging from ear to cheek.* **Bottom center** *Half Mohican hairstyle and half skinhead.* **Left** *Punk couple, the boy wearing a Sex Pistols T-shirt.* **Right** *Punk girls posing for a photograph. Swastikas were used to shock, as were Nazi looking leather caps. With the exception of skinheads, they rarely indicated an affiliation with extreme right wing politics.* **Below** *Punks. These all date from c. 1976, but it is difficult to be precise as there are many punks still faithful to the original styles up to the present day.*

159

UNISEX AND MENSWEAR

Left Men wearing patterned jumpers, Oxford bags and platform soled shoes, 1973. This fashion was widely worn by both men and women.

Above Unisex harlequin patterned coats, designed by Jacques Esterl, Paris, 1970.

Left "His and Hers" V-necked woollen pullovers in green and beige, 1973. This style was also fashionable in the 1920s. **Above** Fashion clothing from the Chelsea boutique Mr Freedom, the interior of which was based on the theme of a ritzy 1940s casino, 1973. **Right** Casual unisex style clothing photographed at a fashion show, c.1976.

CHILDREN

Left An example of the range for winter 1978 by chain store Boots. This shows the sort of practical, reasonably priced children's clothes that characterized the 70s.

Top right These French designs of 1975 show how closely children's clothes and hairstyles follow adult fashion — flared trousers and open neck shirts for the boys, frilled collars and natural fabrics for the girls.

Top right The casual feel to children's clothing in the 1970s is seen here in the use of bright colors, appliqued motifs and braided trims, and floral prints.
Bottom left Denim dungarees and T-shirts were widely worn by men, women and children throughout the 1970s. **Bottom right** Girls' fashion of 1972. The sailor dress on the far right parodies Shirley Temple styles of the 1930s, just as Biba parodied Hollywood styles for adults.

163

HAIR AND ACCESSORIES

Above *Skimpy lace underwear by Lejaby, 1975.* **Top right** *Short, bleached hairstyle, 1979.* **Right** *Thea Cadabra handmade shoes, 1979. Working fulltime, this young shoemaker made two pairs of shoes and one experimental prototype a month.*

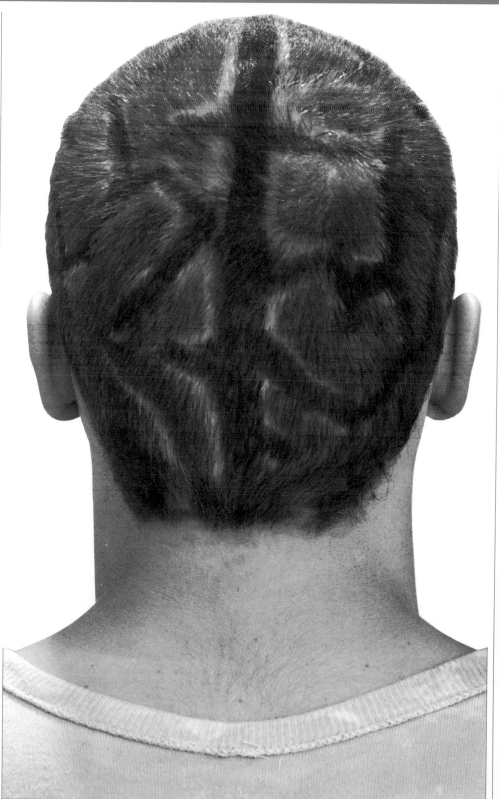

Left Elaborate skinhead hairstyle by Raymond Bird of Alan's in the Kings Road, Chelsea. The average price for such a cut was £30.00 for a seven-hour session. **Top right** Women's hats designed by Edward Mann, 1971. **Right** Cheap plastic fashion jewel ry like this has been worn by many since the late 1970s. **Below** Punk-inspired haircut — known as The Brush — by top hairdresser, Vidal Sassoon, 1972

165

Women's suit by chain store Next, 1988.

CHAPTER·NINE
1980s

To date, fashion during the 1980s has been more pluralistic than ever before. The most noticeable shift in style is from the loose shapes favored during the early 1980s to the more fitted and waist — accentuating designs currently in vogue. The most dramatic development in dress design this decade, however, has been made by the Japanese.

During the 1980s Japanese dress designers have introduced a startling and exciting new fashion force to the catwalks and greatly influenced everyday dress. Japan industrialized in the late nineteenth century and from this period onwards became increasingly receptive to European styles — be it of eating or dress — which were seen to represent progress. Although the Japanese welcomed aspects of Western culture, they have never discarded their own, and in fact have combined the best of both worlds. This trend is particularly evident in the clothing created by their fashion designers, who have repeatedly used the kimono as a starting point.

Japanese designers have rarely made a name for themselves in their own country, where the wealthy domestic consumer demands European — and particularly Parisian — labels. The Japanese did not propose Tokyo as a new fashion capital, but instead went to Paris to establish themselves, as so many designers had done before them. Indeed, as Peter Hillmore emphasized in *The Observer* in 1982, "Paris is an event, like Wimbledon or Henley. It matters not whether the fashion centre of the universe has moved on to Milan, New York or wherever; when people think of fashion they still think of Paris"[1].

Although Kenzo received some acclaim during the 1970s, his garments were largely designed along Western lines. Issey Miyake during the same period, however, injected radical new ideas into fashion having studied couture under Guy Laroche in 1968, the year of the Paris student uprisings. In 1970, Miyake independently created "Peeling Away to the Limit," which consisted of wrapping the figure in a long, narrow strip of fabric and then unwinding it until the naked body was revealed. By reducing body covering to its most basic, Miyake questioned the role of fashion and what exactly constituted acceptable modes of dress. By the early 1980s, a number of Japanese designers started to show their collections in Paris. Rei Kuwakubo, who had worked as a textile and freelance fashion designer, formed the significantly French named Comme des Garcons company in Japan in 1969. During the current decade Rei Kuwakubo, Yohji Yamamoto, Issey Miyake and Kansai Yamamoto are among the leading Japanese designers who have markedly changed the face of fashion.

These designers have created layered, loose fitting and skillfully cut garments, which are predominantly made from wools, silks, cottons and linens in navy, gray, black, tan, and sometimes white and cream. These are often roughly woven and while the colors are largely dull, the surface texture is not. Rei Kuwakubo, for example, uses exciting combinations of velvet mixed with hand cut cord, or cotton woven with wool, and makes much use of crumpled fabrics. The skill of their cut is accentuated when the wearer moves and has, ironically, been carefully contrived to give a look of disarray. Many designs are influenced by traditional Eastern and Western working clothes and the garments worn by the poor. *Vogue* described Yohji Yamamoto's winter 1983 collection as reminiscent of, "...the ruched black and blue urchins, Artful Dodgers and twentieth-century waifs in stretched fisherman's jerseys, mixed-up T-shirts, Dickensian pinstripes and twisted stiff collars."[2] While the intricacy of many Japanese designs is difficult to reproduce for the mass market, their choice of colors, fabrics and pyjama-shaped styles has been widely adopted.

In 1982 Rei Kuwakubo's post-Hiroshima look made a tremendous impact. Suzy Menkes, fashion editor of *The Times*, described this dramatic fashion show: "Down the catwalk, marching to a rhythmic beat like a race of warrior women, came models wearing ink black coat dresses, cut big, square, away from the body with no line, form or

Above
David Bowie has continued to be a fashion influence on the young throughout the 1970s and 80s. He is pictured here at the major cultural/media event of the decade, the fund-raising Live Aid concert of 1985.

Above right
Since Katherine Hamnett started her own company in 1979 she has produced designs aimed at active women. Her range of slogan T-shirts was extensively copied (as she intended it to be), proclaiming her views on political issues such as nuclear disarmament; here, "Stay Alive in '85."

Left
The Princess of Wales, in her famous wedding dress, 1981, by the Emmanuels.

Above
Joan Collins, star of American TV soap opera, Dynasty, is pictured here attending a film première, 1987.

recognisable silhouette...A skirt is a T-shirt, the dangling arms sashed around the hips. Over it goes a real T-shirt in wool jersey, cut asymmetrically, perhaps with a piece of splash printed black and white fabric tied to the shoulders. From the soles of her rice paddy slippers or square toed rubber shoes to the top of her rag-tied hair (lower lip painted a bruised blue), this is a creature from a race apart."[3] The Japanese combine their flair for clothing design with great showmanship, which has assured them extensive press coverage.

In stark contrast to Japanese dress, the elaborate clothing worn in the internationally transmitted soap operas *Dynasty* and *Dallas* has had some impact upon dress in the 1980s. Their actresses, today's equivalent of the 1930s screen stars, promoted the fashion for exaggerated padded shoulders during the first half of the decade. The garments worn by the much publicized Princess of Wales have also had considerable influence upon conventional smart and evening wear; Elizabeth and David Emmanuel, who created the Princess's wedding dress in 1981, are among the many designers who are currently creating nostalgic evening dresses for the rich. Sarah Mower, associate editor of *Vogue*, described some of the most recent fashions which totally reject punk and Japanese styles (although these also remain very popular): "The current sexy doll, high colour, very expensive fashion inspired by Christian Lacroix is almost certainly opposite in its insolent challenge to all the salient features of what went directly before. With the Right in power, this is the perfect right-wing look, reveling as it does in luxury, elitism and traditional versions of decorative femininity."[4] In 1986 Vivienne Westwood designed the eccentric mini-crini, which has since been taken into the realms of more conventional high fashion by Lacroix. These styles offer conspicuous, escapist and glamorous dress to a minority.

During this decade, wealth is increasingly being held in the hands of a few and as a consequence the couture and *prêt-à-porter* industries for both adults and children are flourishing, as are all the luxury trades. In spite of this, numerous leading designers are more than ever before licensing their names to enormous ranges of mass market goods. Many such items, like Dior stockings, retail at similar prices to those in the local stores. These goods have the advantage of prestigious connections — however far removed — to the luxury world of couture, and so the department stores are being forced to upgrade their images. Furthermore, the high fashion impetus of the very successful Next outlets has given the other chain stores considerable competition. Next, whose clothing is targeted at the 25-45 age group, opened its womenswear shops in 1982, menswear in 1984 and introduced children's clothing in 1987. From the outset Next has placed great emphasis on clarity of display and color coordination, and has forced other manufacturers onto the defensive —

Above and **Right**
Paul Smith's menswear features subtle variations on traditional shapes and colors to produce clothes that are interesting but never outrageous. He has exerted a major influence upon the design of all levels of menswear.

Left
Issey Myake designs of 1984, featuring textured weaves; fabric textures are important in much of contemporary Japanese design.

Top right
In contrast to the sweetly feminine image of Princess Diana, or the sexily glamorous Joan Collins, a more active image of woman is seen at the Greenham Common US Air base, which has been the scene of numerous demonstrations by women against the presence of nuclear weapons.

hence Marks and Spencer, in spite of the fact that their clothing sales represent one fifth of the British total, are currently advertising in the society magazine *The Tatler*. Likewise Richard Shops, whose middle range goods have recently been given a facelift by Conran Associates, are advertising in *Vogue*. This is a very new trend and one of major importance to the clothing industry.

In recent years a small section of the trade has begun undergoing a technological change as dramatic as the introduction of the sewing machine. Computer Aided Design (CAD) is being introduced into the design process, as both laying and cutting, the traditional skills of the pattern cutter, can now be worked by the computer. Cutting devices, such as the Eastman and the bandknife, can be programmed and the use of sewing machines can also be enhanced through microprocessor-based controls. These make high quality more easily and quickly obtainable. The industry's uptake of CAD will no doubt take many years and will only ever be introduced into the largest establishments. The vast majority of production units continue to employ less than 50 workers and rely heavily on homeworkers. The fashion industry has always been a labor, rather than capital, intensive industry and will doubtless remain so.

[1](Hillmore, Peter, *The Observer Review*, 24.10.82.)
[2](*Vogue*, 9.83.)
[3](Menkes, Suzy, *The Times*, 22.03.82.)
[4](*The Sunday Times Fashion Supplement*, 6.3.88.)

DRESSES

Below Dior dress with dropped waistline, summer 1980. **Top right** Jersey mini dress by Azzedine Alaia, summer 1987. This style has been very popular and widely copied. **Right** Half mini, half long dress by John Galliano, 1987.

Below Beige cotton and linen dress by Marks & Spencer, summer 1988. The choice of models and styles of garments that Marks & Spencer are currently retailing are aiming to entice a more discerning and fashion conscious customer. The design of this garment is timeless, but more appealing than those of previous years.

Left Classic and very fashionable floral summer dress by Next, summer 1988.

SUITS

Left Neutral colors and simple shapes for 1987. **Below** Sophistication in black leather by Yves St. Laurent, 1984, whose career has hardly faltered since 1962.

Opposite page. Left Citrus colors for Jean Muir, 1986. **Top right** Guy Laroche started his own label in 1957. This 1982 style features an exaggerated shoulder line. **Far right** American designer Calvin Klein is known for his simple shapes which have been widely influential on chain stores such as Next. This suit is from 1984. **Bottom right** Karl Lagerfeld took the helm at Chanel in 1983. His witty interpretations of the classic Chanel suit are much copied: here it is in black denim for 1984.

COATS

Left *Heavy coat designed by Jeff Banks for the Warehouse Utility Clothing Company, 1983. Ankle length boots were widely worn during the early 1980s and these hairstyles have been fashionable throughout the decade.* **Right** *Winter coat by George Armani, for winter 1986/87.*

Right Winter coat and classic, tailored trouser suit by Ralph Lauren, winter 1984-85. **Top right** Mini-crini-style evening coat by Bill Blass, spring 1988. **Bottom right** Loose and unconventional coat dress by Comme des Garçons, winter 1983-84.

EVENING DRESS

Left Floral mini-crini dress with separate sleeves by Christian Lacroix, summer 1988. **Above** Princess of Wales, 1987.

Opposite page. Top right Egyptian influenced dress by John Galliano, summer 1986. **Bottom right** Dress by Jean Paul Gaultier, summer 1987. Gaultier derives much of his inspiration from London street fashion, especially punk, which he glamorizes for the Paris catwalks. **Far right** Turquoise and yellow evening outfit by Jasper Conran, summer 1987.

179

CASUAL WEAR

Left Ralph Lauren is best known for his upmarket interpretations of classic American sports- and workwear, as in this stonewashed denim jacket. **Below** Black denim jeans and jacket by American designer Norma Kamali, 1986.

Right The re-emergence of the mini-skirt. **Top right** Cotton and wool jersey leggings have provided a very popular and comfortable alternative to jeans. **Far right** (bottom) Blue denim jeans, in a baggy shape teamed with oversized jackets, London 1987. **Bottom right** 1980s street fashion, Parisian style.

SEPARATES

Left Mixed check suit by Armani, summer 1987. Armani's garments are always beautifully cut and are often of a timeless design. **Top center** Casual London clothing, 1987. **Bottom center** Perry Ellis, summer 1984. **Right** Thierry Mugler's padded shouldered sports-style suits, winter 1984. As a result of the 1980s fitness craze, tracksuits and leggings have become widely worn for casual wear and have become an alternative to jeans. Mugler has exaggerated tracksuit styles, even to the point of aggression.

Top left Separates by Next, summer 1988. **Bottom left** Vivienne Westwood, 1983, controversially introduced underwear worn over outer garments. **Right** Marks & Spencer separates, summer 1988.

MEN AND CHILDREN

Left Upmarket designs for children by Betty Jackson, 1987.
Bottom left The popularity of hip-hop music in the late 80s has spawned its own style, based on American casualwear and sportswear. **Right** Polyester/cotton mix jacket for boys from chain store British Home Stores, 1984.

Left The Italian suit enjoys a high reputation in the 1980s, here illustrated by one of its leading designers, Gianni Versace. **Below** More Italian menswear: casual separates by Ferré, 1987.

Left A simplified line for a two-piece suit by Issey Miyake, 1987.

HAIR AND ACCESSORIES

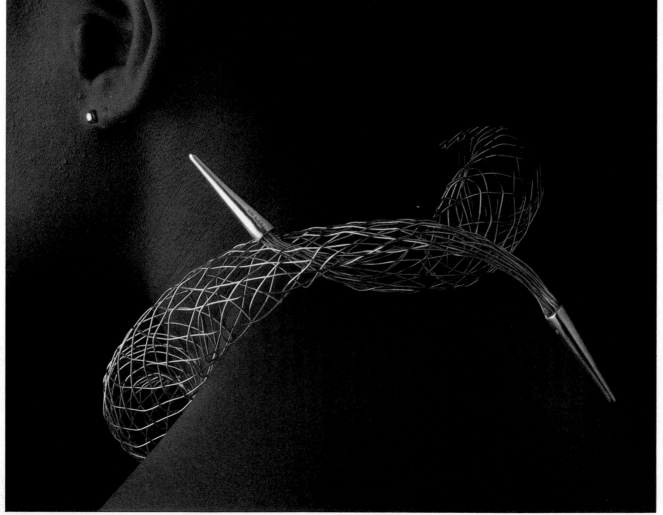

Top left Hairdressing photograph, 1987. Long and short hairstyles for men and women currently offer a great variety of choice. **Above** and **left** A selection of Paul Smith's shoes for men, and the interior of the Paul Smith shop in Covent Garden, London, 1988. Cheaper copies of these traditionally-styled cabinets have recently appeared in many men's clothing shops. Boxer shorts, which can be seen in the display case on the right, have been very fashionable in patterned fabrics for men throughout the decade. **Left** Experimental necklace, c. 1986.

Right and **Far right** These hairstyles have been fashionable in recent years. **Top left** Fashion earrings, c.1986. During the 1970s and 80s, many jewellery designers have adopted an exciting and experimental approach to their work.

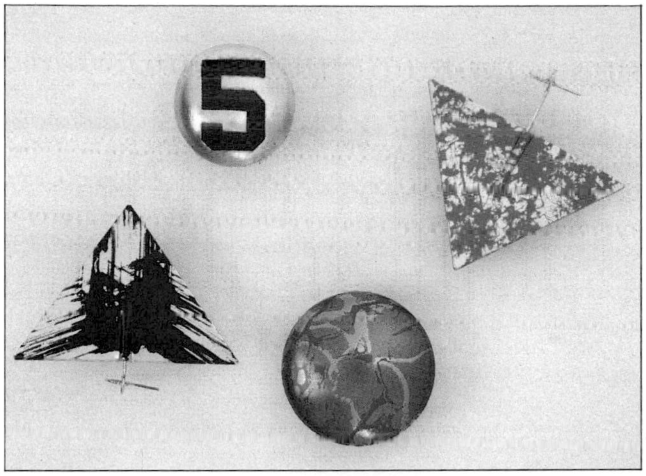
5

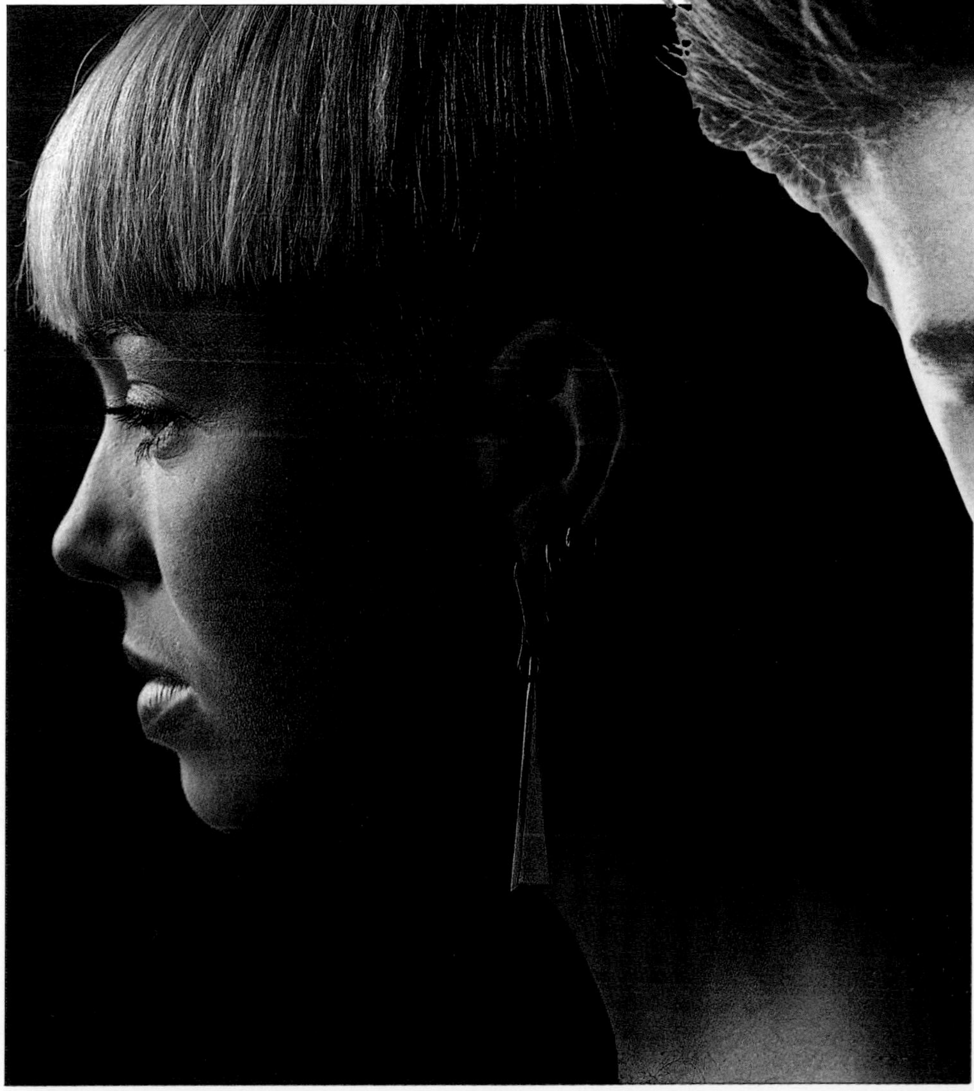

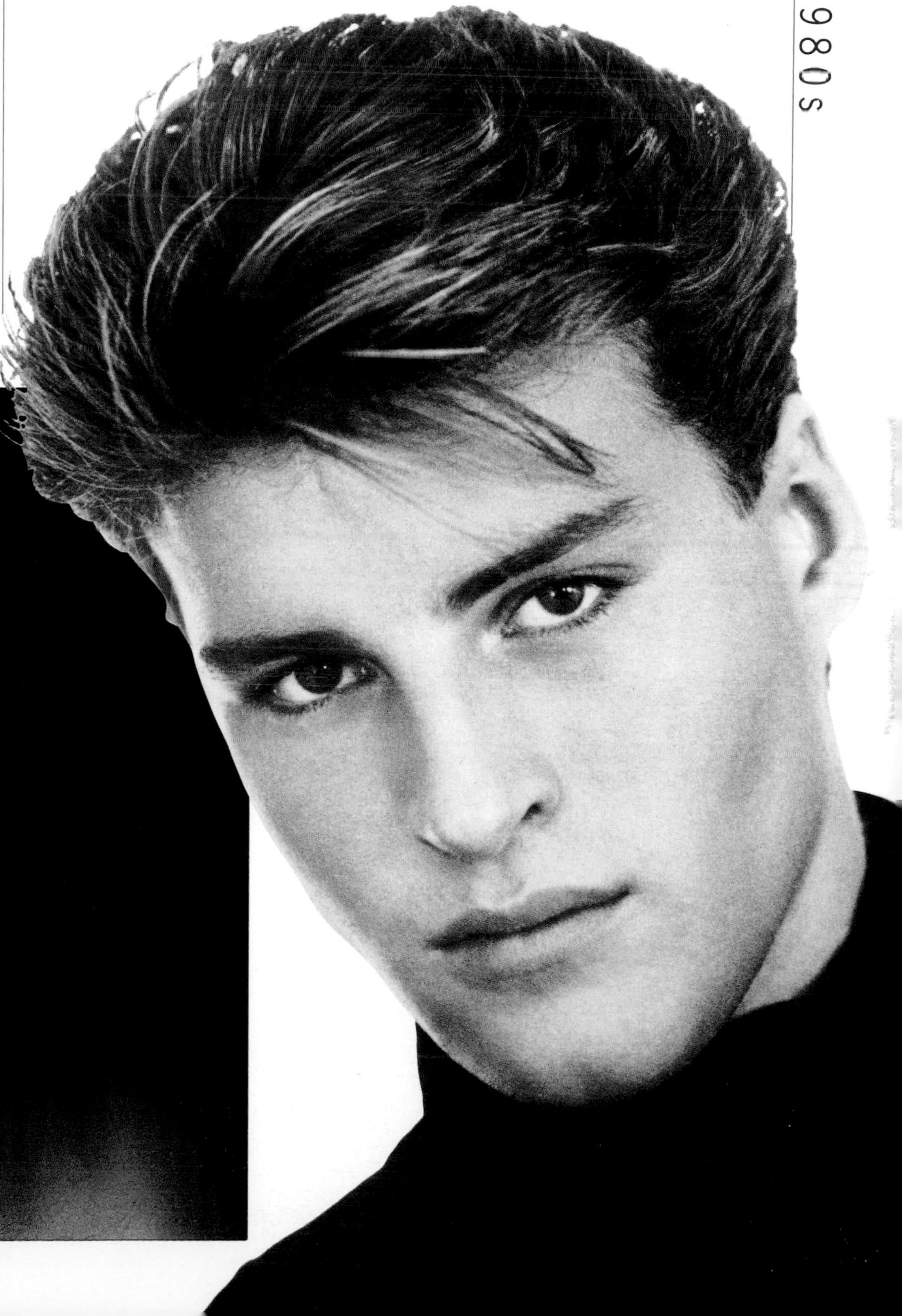

INDEX

Page numbers in *italic* refer to the illustrations and captions

A

"A" line, 100
accessories:
  Edwardian, *28-9*
  1920-1929, *58-9, 62-3*
  1930-1939, 66, *78-9*
  1940-1949, *84*
  1970-1979, *164-5*
  1980s, *186-7*
Adele of California, *105*
Adrian, *67*, 68, 69
advertisements, *45*
African art, 48
Alaia, Azzedine, *172*
Alan's, *165*
Alexandra, Queen, *18*
Alexon, *126*
Alix, 66
Allen, Woody, *157*
American *Vogue*, 13, 34-6
Amies, Hardy, 101
ankle socks, 82
Annie Hall, *157*
Anuszkiewicz, Richard, 122
Aquascutum, *40*
Armani, Giorgio, 149, *176, 182*
Art Deco, *39*, 48, *49, 51*, 146
Art Nouveau, *24, 25*, 146
Ascot, *52, 78, 127*
Ashley, Laura, 146
Aurilan, 100
Avedon, Richard, 101
The Avengers, 128

B

Baby Dior, *139*
Bailey, David, *156*
Bakst, Leon, 34, *36*
Balenciaga, 69, 101, 124
ballet shoes, 85
Ballet Russes, 9, 34, *35, 36*
Balmain, House of, *134*
Balmain, Pierre, 101, *105*
Banks, Jeff, *153, 176*
Banlon, 100
Banton, Travis, 68
Barbier, Georges, 37, *39*
Bardot, Brigitte, 100
Bates, John, *128*
bathing suits, *58, 59*
Bazaar, *14*, 103
beach pyjamas, *59*
beachwear, *76-7, 94-5, 117*
beading, *57*
Beatles, *123, 140*
Beatniks, *111*
Beaton, Cecil, 34, 48
Beer, *55*

Bender, Lee, *150*
Benois, Alexandre, 34
Berard, Christian, 66
Bergdorf Goodman, 9
Berketex, 101, *109*
Best, Alistair, 147
bias-cut dresses, 66
Biba, 122, *123, 129, 131*, 146-7, *147, 163*
Bird, Raymond, *165*
Blass, Bill, *177*
blazers, *140*
Bloomers, *21*
blouses, 21, *25, 28*
Board of Trade, 82
boater hats, *74*
body paint, 125
Body Shop International, 146
Bohan, Marc, *127, 130*
Bond, James, *137*
boots, *153, 162, 176*
Bow, Clara, *49*
Bowie, David, *168*
boxer shorts, *186*
Brando, Marlon, 100, *115*
bras, 48, 100, *115*
Bri-Nylon, *128, 132*
"Bright Young Things", 50
Brissaud, Pierre, *61*
Britain:
  boutiques, 122
  haute couture, 9
  home dressmaking, 50
  1950-1959, 100, 101
  punk, 148
  ready-to-wear clothing, 50
  World War II, 82-3
British Home Stores, *184*
British Land, 147
Burberry, *40, 135*
Burlington House, London, 66
Burne-Jones, Sir Edward, 37
Bus Stop, *150*
bustles, 12, 69
Butterick, 122

C

Cadabra, Thea, *164*
Callot Soeurs, 19
cami-knickers, 77
Campbell-Walker, Fiona, *119*
Cappuci, 149
cardigans, *131*
Cardin, Pierre, *125, 129*, 138
Carnaby Street, London, 101, 125, *140*
Carnegie, Hattie, 9
casual wear:
  1950-1959, *112-13*
  1960-1969, *132-3*
  1970-1979, *156-7*
  1980s, *180-1*
cat-suits, *126*
CC41, 82
Cerruti, Nino, 149
Chambre Syndicale de la Couture

Parisienne, 36
Chanel, 9, 48-50, *55*, 73, 100-1, *175*
Chanel No 5, 49
Chase, Edna Woolman, 13, 34-7
"Chelsea Set", 103
chemise dresses, 100
chemises, *59*
children's clothing:
  Edwardian, *30-1*
  1920-1929, *60-1*
  1930-1939, *74-5*
  1950-1959, *114*
  1960-1969, *138-9*
  1970-1979, *162-3*
  1980s, *184*
  retail outlets, 14
  working class, *12-15*
chokers, pearl, *18*
Churchill, Sir Winston, *55*
Clarendon, Lady, 19
Clarke, Ossie, 122, *151, 154*
cloche hats, *55, 62*
coats:
  children's, *60*
  Edwardian, *22-3, 28*
  1908-1919, *35, 40-1*
  1920-1929, 49, *54-5*
  1950-1959, *104-5*
  1960-1969, *123, 130-1*
  1970-1979, *152-3, 160*
  1980s, *176-7*
Cocteau, Jean, 9
Colliers magazine, 21
Collins, Joan, *169*
Colman, Ronald, *61*
Comme des Garçons, 168, *177*
Computer Aided Design (CAD), 171
Conran, Jasper, *179*
Conran Associates, 171
Le Corbusier, 68
Corole line, 69
corsets, 18, *18*, 21, *28*, 34, 48, *137*
cosmetics, 82, 122
Courrèges, André, 124
Courtaulds, 77, *138*
Courtelle, *126*
couture clothes, 8-12
Coward, Noel, *49*
Craft Revival, 146
Crawford, Joan, 66, *67*, 69, *90*
Crimplene, *151*
crinolines, 37, 69, *109*
Cubism, 48
cycling, *21*

D

Dacron, *133*
Dahl-Wolfe, Louise, *88*
Daily News Sweated Trades Exhibition, 21
Dali, Salvador, 66
Dallas, 170
dancing, 48, *111*
Davies, Gina, *118*
day dresses:
  Edwardian, *24-5*

1908-1919, *38-9*
1920-1929, *52-3*
Dean, James, 100, 102, 148
Debenhams, 101
debutantes, 69, *107*
Delphos dresses, 37, *42*
demob suits, 87
denim, *83, 88*, 100, 102, 147-8, *180*
department stores, 9, 13, 14, 69
Depression, 66
Design magazine, 147
"designer jeans", 148
Diaghilev, Serge, 34, *36*
Diana, Princess of Wales, *169*, 170, *178*
Dietrich, Marlene, 66, *70*
Dior, Christian, 69, 85, *89, 93*, 100, *105, 107, 108*, 124, *127, 130*, 170, *172*
Dior Boutique, *150*
Dr No, *137*
Doeuillet, *35*
Dolcis, 79
Dollar Princesses, 19
Dorazio, Piero, 122
double-breasted suits, *61*, 69
Doucet, Jacques, 19, 34
drainpipe trousers, 102
Drecoll, 19
Dress Carlton suits, *31*
dress suits, *31*
dresses:
  1920-1929, 49
  1930-1939, *70-1*
  1940-1949, *89, 92*
  1950-1959, *106-7, 112, 114*
  1960-1969, *128-9*
  1970-1979, *150-1*
  1980s, *172-3*
  utility, *86*
Duff-Gordon, Lady (Lucille), 19
dummies, 19
dungarees, 102, 148, *157, 163*
Dynasty, 170

E

Eastman cutters, 82, 171
Ecole Martine, 36, 37
Edward, Prince of Wales *see* Windsor, Duke of
Edward VII, King of England, *30*
Edwardian age, 18-21, *22-31*, 101
Egyptian art, 48, *51, 52, 179*
Elizabeth II, Queen of England, 69, *107, 109*
Ellesse, *141*
Ellis, Perry, 148, *183*
embroidery, 9, *41, 43*
Emmanuel, David, *169*, 170
Emmanuel, Elizabeth, *169*
Esterl, Jacques, *160*
ethnic influences, 125, *125, 147, 150, 155*
etiquette, 18
Etiquette for Men, 18
Eton suit, *31*
Eugénie, Empress, 8, 69
evening wear:
  Edwardian, *26-7*

1908-1919, 42-3
1920-1929, 49, *56-7*
1930-1939, 69, *72-3*
1940-1949, *90-1*
1950-1959, *108-9*
1960-1969, *123, 134-5*
1970-1979, *154-5*
1980s, 170, *178-9*
Esthetic dress movement, *24*, 34
Exposition des Arts Décoratifs et Industriels Modernes, Industriels Modernes, Paris (1925), 48
Expressionism, 48

F

fabrics:
  Bri-Nylon, 128, 132
  Courtelle, *126*
  Crimplene, *151*
  Dacron, *133*
  denim, 83, *88*, 100, 102, 147-8, *180*
  Fortuny, 37
  jersey, 49
  linen, 149
  mohair, *113*
  nylon, 100, *114*
  rationing, 82-3, 85
  rayon, 50, *77, 91*
  silk, 49, 50
  stretch-towelling, *126*
  synthetic fibers, 50, 100, *110, 114*
  terylene, *114*
  Tricel, *129*
factories, 21
Fair Isle jumpers, 50, *60*
Farley, Lillian, 13
Fath, Geneviève, *109*
Fath, Jacques, *92*, 101, *104, 109*
Fauvism, 48
Fellowes, Mrs Reginald, 66
Ferre, *185*
film stars, 66-9, 102
Filmfair, 69
Fiorucci, 149
Fitz-Simon, Stephen, 122
flared trousers, 147, *157*
Fontana, 149
Fortuny, Mariano, 37, *42*
fox fur, *39*
France, 8-12, 66
French, John, 101
Funny Face, 103
furs, *39, 40*, 55

G

Gable, Clark, 69
Galliano, John, *172, 179*
Garbo, Greta, 66, 69
"Garçonne Look", 48, 69
Gaultier, Jean Paul, *179*

La Gazette du Bon Ton, 35, 36-7, 38, 39, 42, 56-7, 59, 61, 62-3
Gee, Cecil, *141*
Geinrich, Rudi, 125, *137*
The Gentlewoman, 19, *22*
geometric styles, *128, 131*
George VI, King of England, *74*
Germany, 82
Gibb, Bill, *154*
Gibson, Charles Dana, 21
"Gibson Girl", 21
Ginger Group, *128, 151, 152*
Ginsburg, Allen, *111*
Givenchy, *103, 134*
glasses, *143*
Glynn, Elinor, *49*
Goalen, Barbara, *119*
Godey's, 10
Gone with the Wind, 68
Grangier, Jean, *61*
Greek influences, 66
Greenham Common US airbase, *171*
Greer, Germaine, 146
Grès, Madame, 66, 82
Gross, Valentine, *35*, 37
Grosvenor, Hon Bertie, 19

H

"H" line, 100
hair:
  Edwardian, *26*
  1920-1929, *62-3*
  1930-1939, *78-9*
  1940-1949, 82
  1960-1969, *123*, 125, *142-3*
  1970-1979, *164-5*
  1980s, *176, 186-7*
  punk, 148, *149*
  Teddy Boys, 101
Hamilton, Richard, 100, *100, 116*
Hamnett, Katherine, *168*
handbags, *62*
harem pantaloons, 34
Hari, Mata, *35*
Harlow, Jean, 66, *79*
Harper's Bazaar, 88, 101
Hartnell, Norman, 9, 69, 82, 101, *109*, 155
hats:
  boaters, *74*
  cloche hats, *55, 62*
  Edwardian, *22-3, 28, 29*
  1920-1929, *62-3*
  1930-1939, *71, 78-9*
  1940-1949, *84, 95, 96-7*
  1950-1959, *118-19*
  1960-1969, *142-3*
  1970-1979, *165*
Head, Edith, 68
head-scarves, 82
hemlines:
  1920-1929, 48, 50, 57
  1930-1939, 66
  1960-1969, 122
  World War II, 82
Hepburn, Audrey, 100, *103*

Hepworths, 101
Hillmore, Peter, 168
Hillyard, Mrs, *28*
hip-hop music, *184*
hippies, *125, 125, 140*
hobble skirts, 34, *36*, 92
holidays, 48
Hollywood, 9, 66-9, *79, 100*
home dressmaking, 50
homeworkers, 21, 171
Horst, 66
hotpants, 146, *147, 156*
Howe, Elias, 12
Hoyningen Heune, 66
Hulanicki, Barbara, 122, *129*, 146-7
Humoresque, 90
Hunt, Peggy, *91*

I

ICI, *151*
Ideal Home Exhibition, *103*
illustrations, 36-7, 48, 66
Incorporated Society of London Fashion Designers, 82
Indian boutiques, 125
Iribe, Paul, 36, 37
Italy:
  menswear, *141, 185*
  punk, 149

J

jackets:
  1920-1929, 55
  1950-1959, *115*
  Norfolk jackets, *44*
  World War I, 37
  see also coats; suits
Jackson, Betty, *184*
Jacqmar, *84*
Jagger, Mick, 125
Jailhouse Rock, 102
James, Charles, *73*, 101
"Jane and Jane", *151*
Japanese designers, 168-70
Jays Ltd, 19, *43*
jeans, 102-3, 125, 147-8, *181*
Jermyn Street, 101
jersey, 49
jewelry:
  1970-1979, *165*
  1980s, *186, 187*
  pearl chokers, *18*
  punk, 148
Jugend, 24
jumpers, 50, *60*, 100

K

Kamali, Norma, *180*
Kayser Bondor, *136*
Kennedy, Jackie, *126*
Kenzo, 168
Kerouac, Jack, *111*
kimonos, 168
Kings Road, Chelsea, 148, *156*
Klein, Calvin, 148, *175*
knickerbockers, *153*
knitwear, 50, *60*, 100
Kuwakubo, Rei, 168-70

L

Lacroix, Christian, 170, *178*
Lagerfeld, Karl, *175*
land Army, *44*
Lanvin, Jeanne, *35, 56, 59, 61, 66*, 124
Laroche, Guy, 168, *175*
Lauren, Ralph, 148, *157, 177, 180*
Lawrence, D H, 120
leather, 100, *125, 130, 135, 174*
Leeds Wholesale Clothiers Federation, *87*
leggings, *183*
Leigh, Vivien, 68
leisure activities, 48
Lejaby, *164*
Lenglen, Suzanne, *59*
Lepape, Georges, *35*, 36-7, *59*
"Let It Rock", 148
Letty Lynton, 67, 69
Levi Strauss, 102, 125
Lewis, Kay, *114*
Liberty, 24
Life magazine, 21
linen, 149
Live Aid, *168*
London, 13, 14, 66, 101, 103, 122, 124, 149
Longchamp Races, *38*
Lord and Taylor, 9, 83
lounging pyjamas, *67*
Lucille, 19

M

Mab's magazine, 50
McCardell, Claire, 83-5, *88, 89*
McLaren, Malcolm, 148, *148*
McNair, Archie, 122
Macy's, 69
Mademoiselle, 85
magazines, 21, *21*, 36-7, *45*, 50, 85
mail order, 15, 50, *112, 116*, 122
Mann, Edward, *142, 165*
Mansfield, Jayne, 101
Marks & Spencer, *14*, 15, *15*, 147, 171, *173, 183*

INDEX

Marty, Charles, 37, *38, 42*
Mary, Queen, consort of George V, *44*
maxi dresses, *129*
May, Major Morris, *87*
media, 122
Menkes, Suzy, 168-70
men's clothing:
   Edwardian, *30-1*
   1920-1929, *60-1*
   1930-1939, *74*
   1950-1959, *101-2, 114-15*
   1960-1969, *123,* 124-5, *140-1*
   1970-1979, *160-1*
   1980s, *171, 184-5*
   retail outlets, 14
   utility clothes, *87*
   working-class, 12-13
Metternich, Princess Pauline de, 8
MGM, *79*
Milan, 14, 149, 168
military influences, *133*
mini-crini, 170, *177, 178*
mini skirts, *127,* 146, *154, 181*
Miss Selfridge, 14
Mr Fish, *123*
Mr Freedom, *161*
Miyake, Issey, 168, *171, 185*
models, 19, 21
Mods, *124,* 125
mohair, *113*
Monroe, Marilyn, 100, *100*
Monsoon Fashions, *150*
Morris, William, 37
Morton, Digby, 82, *97*
mourning dress, 21
movies, 66-9, 102
Mower, Sarah, 170
muffs, *22, 23, 104*
Mugler, Thierry, *183*
Muir, Jean, *151, 175, 181*
multiple stores, 14, 15, 101, 122, 170-1

N

Napoleon III, Emperor, 8
Nast, Condé, 21
naval-style clothes, *31*
"New Edwardians", 101
New Look, 85, *92-3, 97*
New York, 13, 14, 66, 69, 168
Newbury Races, *78*
Newton, Helmut, *154*
Newton, Kate, 19
Next, 14, 170-1, *173, 174, 183*
Nichols, Harvey, *70*
nightwear, *77*
Norfolk jackets, *44*
nylon, 100, *114*

O

The Observer, 168
Op Art, 122, *122, 134*

Oriental styles, 34, *42-3*
Orlon, 100
outworkers, 21
overalls, *83*
Oxford bags, 50, *160*
Oxfordshire, 12

P

padded shoulders, 69, 170
Padelford, Miss, 19
Page, Anita, *62*
Painted bodies, 125
Pankhurst, Emmeline, *50*
pantie-girdles, *137*
Papanek, Victor, 146
Paquin, 19, *23, 35, 37, 39, 42, 90, 108*
Paris, 19
   copies of couture models, 13-14
   development of couture industry, 8-12
   *Exposition des Arts Décoratifs et
   Industriels Modernes,* 48
   Japanese designers, 168
   New Look, 85
   1930-1939, 66
   1940-1949, *97*
   1950-1959, 100-1
   1960-1969, 124
   in World War II, 82
Paris Chamber of Commerce, 34
Paris Exhibition (1937), *66*
Parnes, Paul, *92*
party dresses, children's, *31*
Patou, Jean, 13, 48-50, *59,* 67-8, *154*
pawnbrokers, 19
pearl chokers, *18*
peasant styles, 125, 146
Penn, Irving, 101
Penney, J C, 122
perfumes, *26,* 49, 101
Perry, Fred, 125
photography, 66, 101
Photoplay, 69
Picture Post, 85
plastics, 149
platform-soled shoes, *160*
Plunket Green, Alexander, 103, 122
Plunkett, Walter, 68
Poiret, Paul, 34, *35,* 36-7, *52*
Pop Art, 100
Pop festivals, *133*
Portobello Road, London, *133*
Power, Tyrone, 69
Pre-Raphaelites, 37, 146
Presley, Elvis, 102
prêt-à-porter, 13, 170
Princess line, 100
Protective Association of French
   Dressmakers, 36
psychedelic patterns, 125
pullovers, unisex, *161*
Punch, 8, 69, 101
punk, 148-9, *148, 153, 158-9, 165,* 170, *179*
Purism, 48

Q

Quant, Mary, *14,* 103, 122, *123, 128, 151, 152, 154*
Quorum, *151*

R

Rabanne, Paco, *124, 125, 130, 135*
Rational dress movement, *21,* 34
rationing, 82-3, *83,* 85
Raymond "Mr Teasy-Weasy", *143*
rayon, 50, *77, 91*
ready-to-wear clothes, 13-15, 48, 50, 66, 101
Rebel without a Cause, 102
reception gowns, 26
Redfern, 19
Rejelan, *61*
Renaissance, 37
retail outlets, 14-15
   boutiques, 15, 103, 122, 125, 148
   department stores, 9, 13, 14, 69
   multiple stores, 14, 15, 101, 122, 170-1
Rhodes, Zandra, 149, *149*
Ricci, Nina, *73, 104,* 124
Richard Shops, 171
Riley, Bridget, 122
Roberts, Robert, 18-19
Rochas, Marcel, 69, 101
Rock'n'Roll, 100, *110*
Rockers, 125
Roger, Camille, *63*
Rogers, Ginger, 66
The Rolling Stones, 125
romanticism, 69
Rosenstein, Nettie, 9
Rosetti, Dante Gabriel, 37

S

sailor suits, *31*
St. Laurent, Yves, 100, *107,* 124, *126, 155, 174*
Salon d'Automne (1912), 37
San Francisco, 37
Sarong, *116*
Sassoon, Vidal, *165*
Savile Row, 101
scarves, 82, *84*
Schiaparelli, Elsa, 9, 66, 69, *73*
Sears Roebuck, 50
Sebastian, Dorothy, *62*
Second Empire, 8
second-hand clothes, 147-8
Sedgley, Peter, 122
"Seditionaries: Clothes for Heroes", 148
Selfridges, 14, *87*
SEM, *36*
separates, 21, 101, *111, 112-13, 128, 132, 181,*

182-3
Seventeen, 85
sewing machines, *9,* 12, 171
"Sex", 148
Sex Pistols, 148, *148, 159*
shirts, *123,* 125
shoes:
   boots, *176*
   1930-1939, *77, 79*
   1940-1949, 83-5
   1960-1969, *123*
   1970-1979, *164*
   1980s, *186*
   platform-soled, *160*
   stiletto heels, *110*
shops, 14-15
   boutiques, 15, 103, 122, 125, 148
   department stores, 9, 13, 14, 69
   multiple stores, 14, 15, 101, 122, 170-1
shorts, *76,* 77, 146, *147, 156*
shoulders, padded, 69, 170
Shrimpton, Chrissie, 122
silk, 49, 50
Simonetta, 149
Singer sewing machines, 9
Siouxsie and the Banshees, *149*
skating, *23*
skirts:
   bustles, 12, 69
   crinolines, 37, 69, *109*
   hemlines, 48, 50
   hobble, 34, *36, 92*
   mini-crini, 170, *177, 178*
   mini skirts, *127,* 146, *154, 181*
   1908-19, 34, *35, 36*
   1940-1949, *89*
   World War I, 37
slacks, *133*
Smith, Maddy, 122-4
Smith, Paul, *171, 186*
snoods, 82
socks, 82
Spain, 37
spectacles, *143*
sportswear, *20, 28-9, 30,* 48, *58-9, 132-3*
Steele, Tommy, *111*
Stephen, John, 101, *140*
Stiebel, Victor, *78,* 82, 101
stiletto-heeled shoes, *110*
stockings, *12,* 50, 69, 77, 82, *83, 86, 136,* 170
stretch-towelling, *126*
suffragettes, *37, 50*
suits:
   Chanel, 100-1
   Edwardian, *22-3*
   men's, 13
   1908-1919, *35, 40-1, 45*
   1920-1929, 49, *54-5*
   1930-1939, *70-1*
   1950-1959, *104-5*
   1960-1969, *126-7*
   1970-1979, *152-3*
   1980s, *174-5*
   utility, *87*
Sunday Telegraph magazine, *130*
sundresses, *107, 112*
surrealism, 66
sweated labor, 21
swimwear:

1920-1929, *58, 59*
1930-1939, *76*
1940-1949, *89, 94-5*
1950-1959, *116-17*
1960-1969, *136-7*
synthetic fibers, 50, 100, *110, 114*

T

Talbot of Paris, *43*
The Tatler, 1/1
Taylor, Robert, 69
technological developments, 100
Teddy Boys, 101-2, *101, 102,* 125
teenagers, 101-3, *102,* 110-11, *114,* 148
Temple, Shirley, *75, 95, 163*
tennis outfits, *28, 59*
terylene, *114*
textiles *see* fabrics
Thaarup, Aage, *78*
Thompson, Flora, *10,* 12
tights, *14,* 100, 122, *128*
The Times, 168-70
Tinling, Teddy, *111, 113, 132*
Tokyo, 168
"Too Young To Live, Too Fast To Die" 148
Townley, 83
tracksuits, *183*
Tracy, Spencer, 69
Le Train Bleu, 9
Tricel, *129*
trousers:
  beach pyjamas, *59*
  drainpipe, 102
  flared, *147, 157*
  jeans, 102-3, 125, 147-8, *181*
  Oxford bags, 50, *160*
  slacks, *133*
  Teddy Boys, 101
tunics, Poiret, 34
turbans, 34, 82, *96*
Turner, Lana, 100
Tutankhamen, *51, 52*
Twiggy, 122-4, *127*

U

underwear:
  1908-1919, *38*
  1920-1929, *59*
  1930-1939, *77*
  1950-1959, 100, *116-17*
  1960-1969, *136-7*
  1970-1979, *164*
  1980s, *183*
uniforms, World War I, 37
unisex, *125, 160-1*
United States of America:
  Depression, 66
  Dollar princesses, 19
  film stars, 66-9
  haute couture, 9
  mail-order catalogues, 50

1940-1949, 83-5
1950-1959, 100
Poiret replicas, 34
Pop Art, 100
ready-to-wear clothing, 50, *53*
Wall Street crash, 50
wartime clothes, 82-3, *88-9*
Usher, Frank, *129*
utility clothing, 82, 85, *86-7*

V

Veblen, Thorstein, 18
Venice, 37
Versace, Gianni, *185*
Vespa scooters, *124,* 125
Vests, *153*
Villa Savoie, 68
Villeneuve, Justin de, *127*
Vincent, René, *58*
Vionnet, Madeleine, *52,* 66, 69, *71, 73*
visiting robes, *39*
Viyella, *86*
Vogue, 13, 21, 37, 76, 85, 101, 168, 170, 171

W

waistlines, 48, 50, 82
walking costumes, *25*
Wall Street crash, (1929) 50
Warehouse Utility Clothing Company, *176*
Warhol, Andy, 124
wartime clothing, 37, *44-5,* 82-3, *86-9*
Westwood, Vivienne, 148, *148, 157,* 170, *183*
The Wild One, 115
Wimbledon, 112
Windsor, Duchess of, *93*
Windsor, Duke of (Edward, Prince of
  Wales), 50, *60, 74, 93*
Winterhalter, Franz Xaver, 69, *109*
Woman's Journal, 70, 73, 77
women's movement, 146
Women's Social and Political Union, 37
Women's Voluntary Service, 83
working class clothing, 12-13
World War I, 34, 37, *44-5*
World War II, 69, 82-3, 102
"World's End", 148
Worth, Charles Frederick, 8-9
Worth, Gaston, 19
Worth, House of, *10,* 19, 34, *56, 107, 108*
Worth, Jean Philippe, 19
wraps, *26*

Y

"Y" line, 100
Yamamoto, Kansai, 168
Yamamoto, Yohji, 168
Yuki, 155

Quarto would like to thank the following for their help with this publication and for permissions to reproduce copyright material.
Key: t=top; b=bottom; r=right; l=left; c=center.

Cover: *c* Niall McInerney; *tl* Quarto; *tr* BBC Hulton Picture Library; *bl,br* The Telegraph Colour Library.

The Keystone Collection: **pp 9, 12, 13, 14**(*br*), **19, 28**(*bc*), **30**(*c*), **35**(*tr,br*), **37**(*r*), **48, 49, 50, 52, 54**(*c*), **58**(*b*), **59**(*tr,br*), **62**(*tl,tr,br*), **69**(*t*), **70**(*l*), **71**(*l*), **74**(*tl,tr,r*), **75, 76**(*t, bl*), **77**(*bl,tr*), **78, 79**(*tl,bl*), **82, 83**(*l,br*), **84**(*l,r*), **85, 86**(*u,br*), **87**(*tl,tc,b,r*), **90, 91, 92, 93**(*l,c*), **94**(*r*), **95, 96, 97, 98, 100**(*tr*), **102**(*r*), **103**(*r*), **104, 105, 106, 107, 108, 109, 110, 111, 112, 113, 114, 115, 116, 117, 118, 119, 123**(*bl,tr*), **124, 125**(*b*), **126, 127**(*tr,br*), **128**(*tr,bc,br*), **129**(*tl,bl*), **130**(*bl,br*), **131**(*tl,bl*), **132**(*tl,bl*), **133**(*tr,br*), **134**(*tr,br*), **135, 136, 138**(*bl,br*), **139, 140, 141**(*tr,br*), **142, 143, 147**(*tl*), **148, 150**(*r*), **151**(*tl,tr,br*), **152, 153, 154**(*l,tr*), **155**(*tr,br*), **156**(*r*), **157**(*bc*), **158**(*tc*), **159**(*tr*), **160, 161, 162, 163**(*br*), **164**(*tl,tr*), **165, 168, 169**(*bl,r*), **171**(*tr*), **172**(*l*), **175**(*tc*), **178**(*r*), **184**(*r*).

The Telegraph Colour Library: **pp2, 51, 120**(*c*), **123**(*tl,tc*), **125**(*tr*), **127**(*l*), **128**(*l*), **129**(*r*), **130**(*tl*), **131**(*r*), **133**(*l*), **137**(*b*), **138**(*tl*), **141**(*l*), **146, 147**(*tr*), **149**(*l*), **150**(*tl,bl*), **151**(*c*), **154**(*br*), **155**(*l*), **156**(*l*), **157**(*t,bl,br*), **158**(*l,bc,r*), **159**(*t,bl*), **164**(*b*), **174**(*l*), **181**(*l,tr*).

Mary Evans Picture Library: **pp10, 11**(*r*), **16, 20, 21, 23**(*tl,bl,tr*), **24**(*l*), **25**(*r*), **26, 28**(*l,br*), **30**(*l,r*), **31**(*l*), **34, 35**(*l*), **36**(*r*), **37**(*l*), **38**(*r*), **39**(*l*), **40, 41**(*c*), **42**(*r*), **43**(*l*), **45**(*l*), **52**(*tc,tr*), **53**(*l*), **55**(*r*), **56**(*t*), **57**(*l*), **58**(*t*), **59**(*tc*), **61**(*l,tr*), **62**(*bl*), **63**(*r*), **70**(*r*), **73, 77**(*tl,br*), **79**(*tr*), **86**(*l*), **94**(*l*).

Niall McInerney: **pp144, 154**(*bc*), **169**(*tl*), **170, 172**(*tr,br*), **174**(*r*), **175**(*l,tr,br*), **176**(*r*), **177**(*l,br*), **178**(*l*), **179**(*tl,bl,r*), **180**(*r*), **181**(*bc,br*), **182, 183**(*bl*), **184**(*tl,bl*), **185.**

The Victoria and Albert Museum: **pp23**(*br*), **24**(*r*), **42**(*l*), **43**(*r*), **45**(*r*), **71**(*r*), **72**(*l,c,r*), **93**(*r*), The Hearst Corporation, courtesy of *Harper's Bazaar*: **pp88**(*l,tr,br*), **89**(*l,r*). Next Collection: **pp24**(*tr*), 166, **173**(*l*), **183**(*tl*). The Marks & Spencer's Archive: **pp14, 15** The Mansell Collection: **pp18, 25**(*tl*), **38**(*l*), **39**(*r*), **44**(*tl*). The Kobal Collection: **pp61**(*br*), **67**(*l*), **68**(*t*), **103**(*l*). Barnaby's Picture Library: **pp56**(*bl,br*), **57**(*r*), **59**(*tl*), **76**(*br*). BBC Hulton Picture Library: **pp101, 102**(*l*), Christian Dior: **p80.** Elsie Clinch: **p63**(*l*). Punch: **69**(*b*), Amy de La Haye: **pp41**(*r*), **44**(*bl,bc,br*), **46, 52**(*br*), **53**(*r*), **54**(*br*). John Grain: **pp25**(*bl*), **60**(*bc,br*). Marks & Spencer: **pp173**(*r*), **183**(*r*). Paul Smith: **p171**(*tl,b*). Bill Blass Ltd: **p177**(*tr*). Ralph Lauren: **p180**(*l*).

We would also like to thank John Clancy and Michael Lowrie Hairdressing, Brighton, for their help. Every effort has been made to trace and acknowledge all copyright holders; Quarto would like to apologize if any omissions have been made.